10-MINUTE
DEVOTIONS
Growing in Jesus

Glen A. Huff

ISBN 978-1-63814-465-6 (Paperback)
ISBN 978-1-63814-466-3 (Digital)

Covenant Books, Inc.
11661 Hwy 707
Murrells Inlet, SC 29576
www.covenantbooks.com

INTRODUCTION

Attention spans are shortening. Instant results are expected. Lengthy sermons, once viewed as entertaining or engaging, are now met with a get-to-the-point attitude. Our minds wander; the cell phone beckons.

The short articles in this book have two primary purposes: (1) efficiently presenting a scripture point (complete with reference citations for those who may be interested in delving deeper) and (2) providing a vehicle for small group discussions—which was the original purpose.

As to the small group application, if you and I make up the body of Christ (1 Corinthians 12:12), then small groups are probably His backbone and vital organs. Christians are designed to function in community. We spur one another into action; we challenge each other's thoughts and priorities. (Hebrews 10:24-5). Small groups are essential for Bible study, accountability, and promoting acts of service.

But absent structure, small groups easily devolve into social clubs. While there is value in visiting with friends, small groups within the body of Christ provide an opportunity for more. Personal growth and collective health of the body can be enhanced through a disciplined small-group program.

The main purpose of this book is to provide a vehicle for small group ministry. Each chapter furnishes a discussion topic, citations to related scripture, and questions for introspection. Originally, each chapter was used as the text for a seven- to ten-minute video clip. The videos, created using the iPhone movie function, were uploaded to YouTube and sent to members of small groups. Copies of those videos are available on the website found at <u>www.10minutedevotion.online</u>. The groups met each week, discussed the topic of that week's video and shared, in confidence, their reflections in response to the questions posed.

Small groups employing the weekly video clips followed a format like the Wesley class meetings. In keeping with Wesley's outline, the first question for discussion by each group member was a variation of "How is it with your soul?" Wesley's question seems to fall flat in today's vernacular. "I'm fine" was the too-frequent response. Therefore, variations of Wesley's initial question became necessary. For example, the leadoff question posed would be, "How have you grown in your relationship with Jesus this week?" or "Where do you sense God to be working in your life?"

The warm-up question is designed to focus reflection inward. Small groups are to encourage personal growth. Personal growth requires introspection and a secure environment within which to openly share. The group is to be supportive and encouraging without attempting to fix one another's problems.

In this book, each short chapter can be used for small group discussion. When bracketed with prayer, the Holy Spirit can lead groups into deeper understanding and appreciation of their role as members in the Body of Christ.

ACKNOWLEDGMENT AND THANKS

Were it not for my dear wife, Linda, none of this would be possible. She has carefully edited everything I have written and has provided insights and perspectives that were greatly needed.

But more than editing my written work, she has completed me. Although I confess to having joked about being a "victim" of my wife and her prayer group, I acknowledge that her persistent prayers have changed me. She has steadfastly offered encouragement and practical advice. God's creation of a suitable helpmate for Adam (Genesis 2:20–23) was no less accomplished for me.

I thank Linda for being present and engaged in my life.

CONTENTS

BAPTISM OF JESUS
Matthew 3:13–17

Today we consider the baptism of Jesus. Baptism, of course, is the ceremonial cleansing: washing away of our sins. The process begins with confession, which is acknowledgment of our sin. The next step is repentance, i.e., changing the direction of our life away from sin. Baptism is an outward sign of an inward decision to change our life course, to avoid sin and to follow the example of Jesus. Why, then, would Jesus ask John to baptize Him? Jesus was already without sin (see, e.g., Hebrews 4:15), and He was the divine Son of God.

That was the dilemma facing John the Baptist. At the outset of Jesus' ministry, Jesus came to John and asked to be baptized. Understandably, John resisted (Matthew 3:14). John had been imploring people to be baptized so that they would be ready to follow the Messiah who was coming. He had promised that the Messiah would be powerful and worthy of the people's veneration. When Jesus presented himself to John, John immediately knew that Jesus was the one. He knew that Jesus was without sin. And he knew that Jesus was the one who later would offer true baptism with the fire of the Holy Spirit and ultimately would pass judgment on the souls of the people (Matthew 3:11–12, Acts 2:1–4, 2 Corinthians 5:10).

People long have speculated about why Jesus presented Himself for John's baptism. Jesus provided the answer. He said, "It is proper for us to do this to fulfill all righteousness" (Matthew 3:15). That explanation was good enough for John. And John therefore agreed to baptize Jesus.

But how was the baptism of Jesus the "fulfillment of all righteousness"? Righteousness means being in right relationship with God. Being in right standing with God requires that our sins be covered with a perfect sacrifice. (See, e.g., the early instructions of Leviticus 16.) Jesus was that perfect sacrifice. The apostle Paul elaborated with this explanation, He "who had no sin [became] sin for us so that in him we might become the righteousness of God" (2 Corinthians 5:21). Jesus was the "lamb of God who takes away the sins of the world" (John 1:29).

When Jesus underwent John's baptism, He was identifying with humankind. He was meeting us where we are. He understood that the starting place for righteousness that leads to eternal life with God is recognition of our sinful nature and repentance. He knew that "righteousness by faith" would occur when we declare, "Jesus is Lord" and truly believe that He overcame the forces of evil and death (Romans 10:6–10). Even though He was without sin and was the Son of God, Jesus was beginning His ministry on earth by assuming his role as the substitutionary sacrifice for the sins of all mankind.

Moreover, when Jesus was baptized by John, "the heaven was opened and...the Spirit of God [was seen] descending like a dove and alighting on [Jesus] and a voice from heaven said. 'This is my son whom I love; with him I am well pleased'" (Matthew 3:16–17). The baptism of Jesus, therefore, included a public display and announcement from Heaven that Jesus was the anointed Messiah and was pleasing to God.

Baptism marked the starting place of Jesus' ministry that culminated in His assuming our sins. Baptism, for us, is the starting place for our discipleship under Jesus, culminating in our righteousness before Him.

The Great Commission identifies baptism as a starting place for making disciples (Matthew 28:19). You and I are commissioned to become disciples and to encourage others to likewise follow Jesus. As we reflect on baptism, consider these questions for introspection:

1. As we remember our baptism—which is the starting place for discipleship—what progress have you made in growing a meaningful relationship with Jesus?
2. Jesus paid the penalty for our sins. How do you demonstrate gratitude for His sacrifice?
3. Baptism ceremonies today often involve three pledges preceding the ceremonial washing: (1) confession of our sinful nature, (2) repentance, i.e., agreeing to change the direction of our life, and (3)

acceptance of Jesus as Lord over every aspect of our life. As we attempt to live out those pledges, which presents the greatest challenge to you? How do you strive to succeed in these pledges of baptism in your everyday life?

The baptism of Jesus, at first blush, appears illogical. Baptism begins with recognition of our sins and making the decision to change course to lead a more godly life. But Jesus' ministry was about fulfilling righteousness for a world of sinners who were unable to achieve righteousness on their own. Therefore, Jesus took on that role in our behalf. He became the perfect sacrifice fulfilling our righteousness. Praise Jesus for His baptism "so that we might become the righteousness of God" (2 Corinthians 5:21).

WHO IS JESUS?

Matthew 16:15

Who do you say Jesus is? When Jesus posed that question to his disciple Peter, the foundation of the church was laid. Peter, the rock upon which Christ would build His church, understood that Jesus was the promised Messiah, the Son of God (Matthew 16:15–18).

Until that time people recognized Jesus as a prophet, a spokesman for God, a spiritual leader, and a good person. Students of scripture sometimes cited Deuteronomy 18:18 as the authority for saying that Jesus was a prophet. That ancient text promised that God would raise up a prophet from among the Israelites. Others of the day believed that Jesus was the reincarnation of the Old Testament prophets Elijah or Jeremiah.

Even today, some who readily recognize Jesus as a prophet or spiritual leader are reluctant to openly acknowledge Jesus as the Son of God. After all, they rationalize, that sounds judgmental; to ascribe divine nature to Jesus could naturally lead to the conclusion that Jesus—to the exclusion of other theologies' gods—is the only way to Heaven.

(And of course, Jesus clearly stated that He is the only way to access God's Kingdom; see John 14:6.)

Answering the question, "Who do you say Jesus is" may be socially incorrect, but it is unavoidable. If we try to dodge the question or settle for a socially correct statement that characterizes Jesus as great but stops short of calling Him divine, that becomes our answer. And whatever we've stated as our answer to the question, "Who do you say Jesus is?" automatically becomes our final answer by the time we take our last breath in this life.

The question posed by Jesus to His disciples was more than idle curiosity. In fact, it is a question that He poses to each of us, and our answer will affect our soul for eternity. We read in Hebrews, "It is appointed for men to die once, but after this the judgment [occurs]" (Hebrews 9:27). The apostle Paul explained, "We must all appear before the judgment seat of Christ" (2 Corinthians 5:10). God has delegated the task of judgment to Jesus. (See John 5:22, 27; Acts 10:42.) And Jesus, reviewing our words and actions (Matthew 12:36) and our secret thoughts (Romans 2:16) will in effect be asking, "Who do you say I am?"

When Peter answered, "You are the Messiah, the Son of the Living God," Jesus responded by giving Peter the keys to the Kingdom of Heaven (Matthew 16:19). The keys to the Kingdom await those who answer like Peter, openly acknowledging Christ as their Savior, the divine Son of God.

We must not be lulled into complacency, thinking that we can be silent about our thoughts of who Jesus is. Jesus revealed that those who openly acknowledge Him as Christ will be openly acknowledged in Heaven, but those who disown Him publicly would be disowned in Heaven (Luke 12:8, Matthew 10:32–33).

So consider these questions for introspection, if you will:

1. Peter's declaration that Jesus was the promised Messiah, the Son of the Living God, separated him from the popular views of the public. How do your views about Jesus separate you from the publicly acceptable views of the day?

2. Openly declaring Jesus as the Son of God and Lord of your life should affect your everyday living. How is your life different today because of your open declaration of who Jesus is?

3. Are you willing to openly declare Jesus as the Son of God and your personal savior, even if that might subject you to public ridicule or contempt? How are you demonstrating that willingness?

In His day, the masses tended to misunderstand who Jesus was. Peter's declaration separated him from the general public. Even today, the public views about Jesus tend to be distorted or greatly understated. And we are in fact judged by our answer to the question, "Who do you say Jesus is?" The public passes judgment during this temporal life, and Jesus passes judgment in our eternal life. There is no middle ground; either you believe that Jesus is God's Son who came to save your eternal soul, or you are swayed by the sentiments of this temporal world. Which is influencing your answer to the question, "Who do you say I am?"

JESUS ACCEPTS US AS WE ARE

Matthew 11:8

When Linda married me more than forty-five years ago, she loved me for who I was. But that did not stop her from working to change my flaws, calm my temper, and alter my outlook on life. I have jokingly said that I am a victim of my wife's prayer group. Change has occurred in my life because of Linda's persistent (and sometimes unexplainable) love for me.

Jesus loves us. He loves us and meets us where we are. He loves us in spite of what we've done or said or thought. He loves even the most wretched sinner. In fact, Jesus remarked that He came to earth for the sake of sin-sick souls (Mark 2:17, Matthew 9:12). "Jesus came into the world to save sinners" (1 Timothy 1:15). But His love is so persistent that He won't let us remain as He found us, content to be sinners.

By nature, you and I are self-centered. Our instinct is to oppose God, often prompted by the social pressures under which we live. All have sinned and have fallen short of God's standards (Romans 3:23). In short, left to our own devices, you and I are destined for Hell. That's why Jesus promised the counselor, God's Holy Spirit, to teach and guide us (John 14:26).

When we accept Jesus' love, we begin a process of transformation. We put on a new self—one that reflects Christ's knowledge and perspective (Colossians 3:10). We are to shed the patterns of this world and be transformed by the renewing of our minds, through reading His word and spending time with Him in prayer and worship (Romans 12:1). Over time the Holy Spirit transforms us into an image ever closer to that of Jesus (2 Corinthians 3:18).

Jesus loves us where we are. He died for us while we were sinners (Romans 5:8). Jesus died for the irreverent, the disobedient, the lawbreaker, and even for the ornery and despicable persons among us. (See Luke 19:10, Romans 5:19, Hebrews 9:14, Galatians 3:13.)

But that is not the end of the story. While Jesus loves us despite our sinful state, that does not mean that He's content with our sinful ways. That does not mean that He's complacent about our living in opposition to God or in defiance of His standards. That does not mean that there are no consequences for our unrepented sin. Recall, for example, Jesus' instruction to the woman caught in adultery, "Neither do I condemn you but go and sin no more" (John 8:11) or His rejection of those who "talked the talk" but lacked a meaningful relationship with Jesus (Matthew 25:45–46). Because of the love of Jesus, Christians shed their old ways and strive to become more like Jesus (see Colossians 3:5–10).

Jesus came as a gift to sinners. Because we have free choice, we can accept the gift of Jesus' love, or we can reject it. Jesus will not force us. If we accept Jesus, if we open and apply the gift of His love, then we become changed persons. By openly receiving Jesus' love, we begin the process of being transformed into His likeness, while resisting conformity to the ways of this world (Romans 12:2). That change is prompted by the Holy Spirit that takes up residence within those who are in relationship with Jesus (1 Corinthians 3:16).

Jesus meets us where we are. But if we accept Jesus for who He is—the Lord—then we become changed persons. His love is a persistent refining fire. He wants us to experience His presence that brings joy, peace, and love, now and forever.

So as we consider Jesus' compassion for us, as we reflect on His ever-present love for us and what difference that makes, consider these questions for introspection:

1. Are there conditions or circumstances in your life that cause you to feel separated from God's love? Will you confess those to God, release them to your past, and strive to change your ways?

2. How are you opening the gift of Jesus' presence in your life? How are you allowing yourself to be transformed into His likeness?

3. Jesus' love does not mean that anything goes. Like a loving parent who works to

redirect his child, Jesus is striving to transform us. In what ways are you currently conforming to the world instead of adhering to God's standards?

Jesus loves every last one of us. He died for all. He was sent so that none would be lost (John 6:39, 18:9). Scripture reminds us that with His blood, Jesus purchased people from every nation, every language, and every walk of life (Revelation 5:9). Jesus accepts us where we are.

But don't let that unmistakable fact confuse you into thinking that Jesus will blithely accept anyone who chooses to remain in sin. Refusing the Holy Spirit's prompting can result in eternal damnation (1 Corinthians 6:10, Revelation 22:15). His love for us is a gift designed to save us, transform us, and bring us to eternal life with our Maker.

JESUS IS GENTLE
Matthew 11:29

Understanding the nature of Jesus is no easy task. The prophets of old described the Messiah in terms that often seemed contradictory and confusing. The Prophet Jeremiah described the Messiah as a strong and forceful person who would execute judgment and righteousness on earth and would save Judah and cause Jerusalem to be safe (Jeremiah 33:15–16). Isaiah said He would bring healing and freedom (Isaiah 42:7). But elsewhere in the Old Testament prophecy, the same Messiah was forecast to be wounded, oppressed, and slaughtered (see, e.g., Isaiah 53:5–7). He was forecast to be gentle: "a bruised reed he will not break, and a smoldering wick he will not snuff out" (Isaiah 42:3).

Context, of course, makes the difference. Scripture describes Jesus in contrasting terms. Jesus is ruler yet is servant; He is healer but afflicts His enemies; and He is judge and He is savior. The characteristics displayed in His first coming differ markedly from those in His second coming.

During His first appearance on earth, one of the words Christ used to describe His nature was "gentle." Here's the passage from Matthew: "Take my yoke upon you and learn from me, for I am gentle and lowly in heart (humble), and you will find rest for your soul. For my yoke is easy, and my burden is light" (Matthew 11:29–30).

When Jesus described Himself as "gentle," he was not suggesting that He was weak, wimpy, or accepting of anything and everything. In the context of this passage, Jesus was contrasting His ways with the onerous requirements imposed by the religious leaders of the day.

When we read the term "yoke," we often visualize the harness structure used on beasts of burden—oxen, mules, horses—so that they can pull heavy loads. But in Jesus' time the word "yoke" also was a colloquialism referring to the shawl worn by religious leaders.

The religious teachers would conjure up rules and regulations to be kept by their followers as requirements for righteous living. These mandates typically were derived from God's principles given to Moses, but they multiplied the strictures for everyday living. These requirements were referred to as the rabbi's yoke—i.e., burdens assumed by adherents of a particular rabbi.

So when Jesus said that His yoke is easy and His burden light, He was saying that those who followed Jesus would not be overburdened by man-made rules and regulations governing everyday life activities like those created by religious leaders of that day. The followers of Jesus would be expected to adhere to God's principles for life but not to the minutia devised by religious leaders. In fact, Jesus instructed that two principles—love God and love one another—summed up all the laws espoused by Moses and the prophets (Matthew 22:40). Of course, loving others does not mean blindly approving godless actions of others because that would lead them to eternal damnation—which is not a loving thing to do (see James 3:1).

Ultimately, Jesus bore our burdens by dying for our sins—there was nothing gentle about that! Jesus covered our sins so that our faith would be counted as righteousness (see Genesis 15:6, Romans 4:20–22, Galatians 3:6). So when Jesus described himself as gentle and humble, He was talking about our righteousness depending, not on adherence to man-made regulations, but simply on having faith in Him. His requirements were easy: "If you declare with your mouth, 'Jesus is Lord' and believe in your heart that God raised him from the dead, then you will be saved" (Romans 10:9). At that point the Holy Spirit leads believers, transforming them into new beings (2 Corinthians 3:18).

The standards imposed in today's culture often conflate Jesus' gentleness with the mistaken notion that no standards apply. That was never the case. In fact, Jesus laid down His life underscoring the importance of God's standards. (See, e.g., Ephesians 5:25–33.) Jesus bore our burdens and opened the path to union with God. So consider these questions for introspection about the gentleness of Jesus:

1. Jesus does not force Himself on us. Because He is gentle, we sometimes find it easy to ignore Him. What steps are you

taking to discipline yourself to take Jesus seriously—to not ignore Him?

2. A gentle spirit can telegraph confidence and strength. We don't need to be defensive or abrasive about promoting Jesus—in fact, that approach often undermines our effectiveness in making disciples. How are you incorporating "gentleness" into your promotion of Jesus?

3. A popular criticism of the church today is that its people are judgmental. How are you explaining God's standards in truth and love without condemning others?

Jesus advanced the Kingdom of God with gentleness and humility. He did not sell short God's principles for daily living, yet He demonstrated Solomon's wise saying, "A gentle word turns away wrath" (Proverbs 15:1). History has proven that no one can succeed in carrying the yoke of righteousness for themselves (Acts 15:10). But when we accept Jesus as Lord over our life, His grace covers us and relieves us from the impossible burden of being perfect. Jesus is gentle, His yoke is easy, and His burden is light.

JESUS IS LOVE
John 13:34–35; 1 John 4:8

Jesus is love. Scripture clearly states that God is love (1 John 4:8) and that God is in Jesus and Jesus is in God (John 14:10–11). The apostle John begins his Gospel message by saying that Jesus—the Word of God—is God. (John 1:1). It is safe to say, therefore, that love—God's nature—is a profound and defining characteristic of Jesus too.

If we are to understand Jesus, therefore, we need to understand His love. Understanding the love of Jesus is made difficult because of our contemporary use of the word "love." In today's culture we say we "love ice cream" or we read "love stories" or we are "swept off our feet by feelings of love."

In our contemporary vernacular we think of love as an emotion—a feeling. But the love of Jesus is a decision. He made the decision to die on the cross for our sake, while we were yet sinners (Romans 5:8). That was love. The apostle John put it this way, "This is love: not that we loved God, but that He loved us and sent His Son as an atoning sacrifice for our sins" (1 John 4:10).

Love, therefore, as characterized by Christ is not a fickle feeling that comes and goes on tides of circumstances of the moment. Love is a decision. It is a commitment to act selflessly, even self sacrificially, for the sake of someone else. G. K. Chesterton put it this way, "To love means loving the unlovable." Jesus taught, "Greater love has no one than this: to lay down one's life" for another (John 15:13).

As disciples of Jesus, we are called to follow His example. We are to make and keep the decision to love others—even the unlovable—and even when we don't feel like it. By this attribute—loving others—we are known as followers of Jesus (John 13:34–35).

In today's world, Christians risk substituting sentiments of warm, cuddly feelings for love. Face it; we don't have warm cuddly feelings for terrorists, child abusers, scam artists, and the like. Yet those are among the people for whom Christ died and those are among the people we are called to love. Jesus set the example. He went to the cross—an act of love—for the sake of reprehensible sinners. He died even before any of us felt remorse or shame for our shortcomings.

Jesus' decision to love was serious—as serious as death on the cross. As followers of Jesus, we must guard against taking His love lightly. Love, for example, does not mean that anything goes—that Jesus loves us, and therefore we should accept or promote ungodly conduct. Such love leads people onto a path that leads to destruction and damnation—the very opposite of Christ's love. Love means that the effects of sin are so serious that Jesus made the conscious decision to die a painful death to cover the sins of those who will become His followers.

When we accept Jesus' sacrifice and declare Him as Lord, our actions should reflect His love. That love includes adhering to His commands (John 14:15). Loving as Jesus loves means standing for His principles and standing for the people for whom He died. That means making His Gospel message available to all who will hear it.

So consider, if you will, these questions for introspection:

1. Loving as Jesus loves means openly obeying His commands. How are you taking a public stance for Jesus?
2. Loving as Jesus loves means reaching out to the "unlovable." How are you promoting Jesus among those whom you find "unlovable?"
3. Loving as Jesus loves means taking self-sacrificing action to reach the people of this world. What self-sacrificing actions are you taking to bring people to Jesus?

Jesus is love. He set a model of sacrificial giving for the benefit of all. Following that example is not easy. But as we transform into the likeness of Jesus, we understand that love is a decision. And when we live as Jesus demonstrated, we are able to resist being tossed about on waves of emotions and feelings, and can speak truth in love (Ephesians 4:14–15).

TRANSFIGURATION

Luke 9:28–36

If ever they doubted the existence of a spiritual realm, those doubts were certainly quashed for the disciples Peter, John, and James at the transfiguration. Like the disciples living at the time of Jesus, we too live in a physical, earthly plane, but the forces of the spiritual realm are constantly at work in our midst.

Just a week before the transfiguration, Jesus revealed to his disciples that he would be martyred but then would rise from the dead "on the third day" (Luke 9:22). In that same message, Jesus slipped in an extra piece of information: "Truly I tell you, some who are standing here will not taste death before they see the Kingdom of God" (Luke 9:27). About a week later, God's spiritual kingdom opened briefly before them during a mountain top time of prayer.

Luke writes that as Jesus was praying, his face and clothes lit up with the brilliance of a flash of lightning (Luke 9:29). Jesus was demonstrating that a connection to God's Heavenly Kingdom is made through prayer.

But there was more. Two men identified as Moses and Elijah also appeared in glorious splendor. The disciples would have known of Moses and Elijah only through scripture; both Old Testament characters preceded the time of Jesus by many centuries. Yet the disciples immediately recognized both men. (Have you ever wondered how we will recognize our distant relatives in Heaven? This passage suggests that in God's Kingdom we will simply know one another.)

Perhaps the most remarkable part of this brief encounter, when God's Kingdom interjected itself into the earth plane, was the topic of discussion. Luke reports that they talked about Jesus' departure that was about to be fulfilled at Jerusalem (Luke 9:31). This was a spiritual huddle among Moses, the deliverer of God's law; Elijah, representing God's prophets; and Jesus, the Son of God who came to restore the relationship between God and his people. The fulfillment would be accomplished by Jesus' sacrifice on the cross at Jerusalem, covering the sins of mankind.

Heaven already knew how it would play out. Events that had not yet unfolded on earth were already known in God's realm. And the bearers of God's law and His prophecies would finally see the narrow gate opened to allow those who believe in Jesus to have eternal union with their Creator. The authorities of Heaven were present supporting Jesus' earthly mission.

Peter, not wanting this mountaintop experience to end, offered to build three tabernacles—or shelters—just as Moses and Elijah were leaving (Luke 9:33). Suddenly the disciples were overcome by God's Shekhinah glory. God's holy presence enveloped them in a cloud, and a voice from heaven announced, "This is my son whom I have chosen, listen to him" (Luke 9:35). And only Jesus was left standing with the disciples.

Years later, long after Jesus ascended into heaven, Peter recalled the event. "We ourselves heard this voice that came down from heaven when we were with him on the sacred mountain" (2 Peter 1:18). And the apostle John explained the significance of the event, "The word (of God) became flesh and made his dwelling among us. We have seen his glory..." (John 1:14).

The connection between God's Kingdom and those of us living on earth seems remote and mysterious. Yet that connection can now be an everyday occurrence, accessed through prayer and manifested by the Holy Spirit that dwells within the hearts of believers (1 Corinthians 3:16).

So what are the faith-application points for us in this passage of scripture? Let's consider these questions:

1. Prayer is our connection directly into the heavenly throne room of God (Revelation 5:8). Knowing that, how should that affect our prayers?
2. God's presence was manifest in a cloud at the transfiguration and at the dedication of Solomon's temple and during the great exodus of the Hebrew nation. Rabbinic literature describes this presence as "Shekhinah glory," meaning God's powerful indwelling presence. God sends His Holy Spirit to dwell in the hearts of believers. Knowing that God's Holy Spirit

lives within us, how does that affect our everyday living?

3. God spoke for all to hear, identifying Jesus as His Son and instructing the disciples to listen—that is to respect and follow his teachings. How do we honor Jesus as the Son of God?

We are spiritual beings living temporarily in the physical world. Our lives are affected by activities in the spirit realm (Ephesians 6:12). Therefore, God has provided us with access to His powerful presence. He's given us the opportunity for connecting by prayer. He's given us the indwelling presence of His Holy Spirit. He's provided hope that comes from knowing that God's Kingdom is at hand and that Jesus is the Son of God.

JESUS USED SCRIPTURE TO COMBAT SATAN

Matthew 4:1–11

O nly a fool would enter an active battlefield without taking some precautions for protection. Yet most of us do exactly that every day. We live in a battlefield. And the enemy, Satan, "prowls around like a roaring lion looking for someone to devour" (1 Peter 5:8).

Satan temporarily has dominion over this world. Paul referred to Satan as the "ruler of this dark world" and the "god of this age" (Ephesians 6:12, 2 Corinthians 4:4). Jesus called Satan the "prince of this world" (John 14:30, 16:11). The apostle John wrote, "the whole world is under the control of the evil one" (1 John 5:19).

God has forewarned us. We are living in a minefield of temptation and sin. Satan actively seeks to inflict mortal wounds on as many souls as he can. The battle rages every day and the casualties are great.

Author Steve Farrar puts it this way. He says that you and I are "point men." That is, our job in life is to know the enemy and his tactics and to master the defenses that have been issued to us, so that we are able to defend against Satan's attacks as we lead our family and friends through the evils that surround us.

How can we possibly navigate this war zone? Jesus demonstrated how.

Just before launching His ministry, Jesus was taken into the wilderness for a time of extreme testing. Satan repeatedly offered worldly rewards if Jesus would worship Satan. Jesus was tired, He was hungry, and He was feeling the weakness and vulnerability that we humans feel each day. This was intense spiritual warfare. Jesus prevailed.

Let's look at how Jesus protected Himself from Satan's challenges during the forty days in the wilderness. His weapon was scripture. Jesus knew the Word of God inside and out. Jesus' knowledge of God's scripture was so complete that the apostle John said that Jesus was the Word of God personified (John 1:14).

In spiritual warfare, God's Holy Scripture is the weapon we've been issued. A good soldier knows his or her weapon thoroughly, and that requires years of training. Learning scripture is a life skill to be taught from an early age and continued throughout our tour of duty on earth. God has instructed us to "impress scripture on our children" and to make scripture a topic of conversation everywhere (Deuteronomy 6:7–9).

In his letter to the Ephesians, Paul described the protective gear issued for spiritual warfare—the helmet of salvation, the breastplate of righteousness, the shield of faith, and the belt of truth. But the only weapon listed was the "sword of the Spirit, which is the Word of God" (Ephesians

6:13–17). To sharpen scripture skills, some churches conduct "sword drills" for their youth—competitions to teach familiarity with scripture.

Satan's surprise ambushes come when we least expect it and when our guard is down. Therefore, our weapon—the sword of God's Word—must constantly be ready for use. And our knowledge of God's Word must be so complete that we are not duped by Satan's subtle twisting of words.

For example, we sometimes hear Satan's agents falsely represent sayings as scripture. "God helps those who help themselves" is falsely paraded as scripture; that does not appear in the Bible. Or spinning the application of God's Word, such as "do not judge." Rather than judging others, we are called to examine our own motives, but we are also required to be discerning, exposing false teachers (Matthew 7:15–20) and exercising guidance and discipline for fellow Christians (1 Corinthians 5:1–2).

Spiritual warfare is pervasive and requires us to confront it with specialized knowledge of scripture and sensitivity for the leading of God's Holy Spirit. As we consider the importance of having scripture always ready for use, consider these questions if you will:

1. What steps are you currently taking to enhance your knowledge of scripture?
2. What steps are you currently taking to teach scripture? (Steven Covey says we learn most thoroughly when we learn in order to teach.)

3. When are you engaging in drills to test your knowledge of scripture? Drill weekends (spiritual retreats) can enhance our adeptness in handling scripture and focused discussions about scripture can likewise be beneficial.

Intimate knowledge of scripture is essential for addressing the spiritual warfare that engulfs us every day. And incomplete knowledge is as dangerous as carrying a loaded pistol without exercising safety steps. Partial knowledge of scripture makes us vulnerable to being tricked by Satan's spin tactics, causing us to unwittingly inflict injury on ourselves or others.

Satan attacks when we are tired, weak, or inobservant. Be ready. Hone your scripture skills. Scripture is the weapon we've been issued for everyday spiritual warfare.

WORSHIP GOD ALONE

Matthew 4:1–11

During Lent, we sometimes focus on the means employed by Christ for handling earthly temptations. His examples are instructive for us as we strive to resist the temptations that are thrust upon us every day.

We know that Jesus fasted, feeding His spirit rather than satisfying human hungers. We've seen that Jesus knew scripture thoroughly so that He could recognize Satan's deceitful ways and respond with the inspired and powerful words of God.

Today, we focus on worshiping the one true God. Scripture tells us that Satan left Jesus, and then God's angels moved in to minister to Jesus when Jesus finally exclaimed, "Away from me, Satan! For it is written, 'Worship the Lord your God, and serve Him only'" (Matthew 4:10, Jesus quoting from Deuteronomy 6:13).

We fall for temptations of this world when we worship other gods, i.e., when we place greater emphasis on things of this world than we place on our relationship with the one true God. Have you ever reached the end of the day and realized that activities of the day have crowded out any time for prayer or scripture study? Those things that get in the way of our "worshipping God and serving Him only" are likely false gods.

Jesus' time of temptation in the wilderness closed when He spoke aloud from the admonition Moses gave as recorded in Deuteronomy 6:13–14: "Fear the Lord your God, serve him only...do not follow other gods, the gods of the people around you." When Moses announced the directive to avoid the gods of other people, he was preparing the Hebrew nation for their entrance into the land that God promised. Even though God would be with them, they would be tempted to follow pagan cultures and religions that were prevalent there. The Canaanite practices of sexual immorality and even infant sacrifice were lurking in the land where God's chosen people would live.

Astonishingly, the peer pressure was too great for God's people, even though they'd been forewarned to guard against adopting the ungodly practices promoted by pagan cultures. Before long, the Canaanite princess, Jezebel, became queen and the Hebrew people were drawn into a culture of sexual immorality, infant sacrifice, and open opposition to God's influence in the world (see 1 Kings 16:31–33).

Today we read the exploits of Jezebel and are shocked to think that God's people would fall for the false gods that Jezebel promoted. But the human need to be accepted by the people around us, even today, exposes us to the very real risk of succumbing to false gods that displace our worship of the one true God.

Infant sacrifice to the god of convenience and sexual relations that defy godly standards are prevalent in our current culture. Even God's people face the temptation to conform to "choice" and political correctness that mandates outright defiance of God's standards for living.

The false gods that plagued the Hebrew nation have not gone away. In fact, they have proliferated. Anything that separates us from worshiping God is a false god—it is interference in the relationship that God seeks to have with his people. Jesus taught that when we are absorbed in worldly concerns—what we shall eat or what we shall wear—"things the pagans run after," we make ourselves vulnerable to Satan's torment and the temptations of peer pressure (see Matthew 6:31–33). Therefore, Jesus encouraged us to "Seek first the Kingdom of God and His righteousness" (Matthew 6:33). Worshiping God and serving Him needs to be our priority in daily living.

As we reflect on prioritizing our worship of God, consider these questions for introspection:

1. What false gods can you identify that dominate the world culture in which we live?
2. What tends to interfere with your daily worship of the one true God?
3. How are you worshiping and serving God in your daily living?

Worshiping God and serving Him starts as a conscious decision. The decision to allow no other gods in our life is so important that it is listed as the very first of the Ten Commandments: "You shall have no other gods before me" (Exodus 20:3). We need a plan of action to counter the peer pressure that attacks us daily—a pressure to conform to Satan's temptations—to live like those around us.

But you and I are not of this Kingdom (John 18:36). As followers of Christ, we do not adhere to Satan's culture. Rather, we live by God's Word and worship and serve Him alone in our daily living.

JESUS IS FOR YOU
Matthew 26:20–35; Luke 22:20

People seem to be in constant search of a "New Deal"— that is, finding a social program that would cure the woes that torment us every day. To date, no political or social solution has proven to be a panacea. But more than two thousand years ago, Jesus offered a new deal that has enabled believers to overcome the deadly consequences of sin and find joy amid the turmoil even in this world.

"This is the cup of the New Covenant," Jesus announced to His disciples. "My blood...poured out for you" (Luke 22:20). We celebrate His New Covenant every time we participate in communion and every time we yield to His leading in our life. His new deal is not a reallocation of material wealth, nor is it a redistribution of worldly power. The New Covenant restores our relationship with God. And that's a new deal that works.

As it turns out, the Old Covenant that temporarily restored mankind's relationship with God through animal sacrifice was a shadow of the New Covenant. Since the wages of sin is death (Romans 6:23), resolution of sins required the sacrificing of life (Hebrews 9:22). But the prophet

Jeremiah had foretold the coming of a New Covenant. The prophet wrote, "The days are coming, declares the Lord, when I will make a new covenant" (Jeremiah 31:31).

The New Covenant was the one announced by Jesus at the Last Supper. Jesus explained that His blood would be "poured out for many for the forgiveness of sins" (Matthew 26:28). Jesus would be the final and lasting sacrifice to cover the sins of mankind. Jesus would be "the Lamb of God who takes away the sins of the world" (John 1:29). Jesus took on our sins so that we would be deemed righteous before God (2 Corinthians 5:21, Romans 5:8).

In the Hebrew language, Jesus' name is Yeshua, a name that means to rescue or save. Specifically, Jesus came to rescue us from the effect of sin, saving our eternal soul from lasting agony of separation from God. Jesus explained that He came to earth so that we could have life and have it abundantly (John 10:10). That abundant living includes experiencing peace and joy even in the midst of earthly pain and suffering (Romans 15:13, Philippians 4:7).

Years ago, I heard a lecturer describe meeting his future in-laws for the first time. He had traveled a great distance and was warmly welcomed into their home. Within minutes of his arrival, he was offered food—"You must be hungry from the trip," they said, "help yourself to anything in the fridge." Then they carried his suitcase to the guest room and helped him settle in. Moments later his future father-in-law handed him the keys to the family car so that he and his fiancée could get around town.

The lecturer pointed out that within a few minutes of his arrival, his future in-laws had provided food, a comfortable room, and even access to the family car. "What caused them to be so generous?" he asked. It was the relationship that he had with their beloved daughter that caused him to be warmly accepted into their home.

God sent His Son, Jesus, to pay the penalty of our sin so that we can stand in righteousness before God. And when we have a relationship with God's beloved son, we are accepted into God's home; we are welcomed with open arms. We are accepted as family, brothers, and sisters in Christ, children of God, beneficiaries of God's plan to restore mankind's original relationship with God. (See John 14:21 "the one who loves me will be loved by my father.")

The relationship we have with Jesus is personal. When we accept Jesus as Lord, we will be saved—welcomed into God's eternal house (Romans 10:9). Our mother cannot make that relationship for us; our pastor cannot make the commitment for us. Our relationship with Jesus is based on our personal connection, yielding to His leadership in our life.

So consider these questions for introspection, if you will:

1. Jesus sacrificed himself for the New Covenant relationship with us. How are you reciprocating, i.e., what are you doing to be in a meaningful relationship with God's beloved Son Jesus?
2. When you take communion, commemorating Jesus' Last Supper, what thoughts

go through your mind? How are you drawn into "communion" with God?

3. In the New Covenant, Jesus asked that the Counselor, God's Holy Spirit, dwell within us. How are you listening for the Holy Spirit to lead you?

Above all, Jesus did not come to condemn us. Satan spins the false narrative that God sent Jesus to spy on us. Nothing could be further from the truth! God is love. God loves us so much that He sent His Son, Jesus, to give His life as recompense for our sins (John 3:16). To that promise the Bible adds, "For God did not send His Son into the world to condemn the world, but to save the world—one person at a time—through Him" (John 3:17).

Through the New Covenant offered by Jesus' sacrifice for our sins, we are welcomed into God's presence. Moreover, we receive the indwelling Holy Spirit to direct us in godly living and an ever-closer relationship with Jesus. The Spirit comforts us in the midst of worldly discord and leads us into the eternal presence of our Maker.

JESUS IS OBEDIENT

Matthew 26:36–46

Nearly every one of us has gone through a phase in life when we wanted to be free—free from having to answer to someone else. Our human nature is to crave independence; we naturally recoil against authority. As a child or teen, we may have resisted parental authority. Perhaps on the job we've defied the boss. But eventually, in the normal process of growing up, we come to realize that structure and answering to authority are foundations for our freedom and success. By contrast, rejection of obedience to godly authority leads to downfall.

The concept of obedience is counterintuitive. Ask the trafficked runaway teen or the homeless drug addict how they became enslaved to a pimp or imprisoned by the need for a fix, and typically (not always but typically) their answer will trace back to someone rebelling against godly authority in their life.

The effect of rejecting or embracing obedience to authority was demonstrated in Jesus' story of the Prodigal Son found in Luke 15:11–24. The younger son yearned to be free from having to obey his father. And so he asked for his inheritance early, left the farm, and squandered everything he'd been given on "free" living.

Of course, it was just a matter of time before the son ran out of money and was trapped in poverty, powerlessness, and shame. When he returned to the structure of his father's world, he found the freedoms that previously had been his when he was living by his father's standards.

The temptation to be disobedient infects us today. Satan whispers, "God's ways are restrictive. Don't you want to be free from God's standards, free from obedience?" All along Satan knows that disobedience to God is the surefire way to become enslaved to sin and separated from joy and relationship with God.

Having to answer to appropriate authority provides structure in our life and tends to make us more responsible in our actions. Striving to obey God's standards is essential for Christians. Even Jesus, who was God (John 1:1), answered to higher authority—God the Father (John 14:10).

Today we focus on Jesus' example of obedience. In particular we focus on the fact that Jesus was "obedient to the point of death...even death on a cross" (Philippians 2:8). On the night of His betrayal, Jesus was aware of the excruciating pain that awaited Him. At the Garden of Gethsemane, Jesus is recorded as having said, "My soul is overwhelmed with sorrow to the point of death" (Matthew 26:38).

Jesus had left the comforts of heaven in order to become the sin offering for mankind (see Luke 2:30, 38).

Following God's plan for salvation, Jesus became one of us, knowing that that would lead to His sacrifice.

Throughout His ministry, Jesus was obedient to God. He explained, "The words I say… I do not speak in my own authority. Rather, it is the Father living in me, who is doing His work" (John 14:10, John 12:49). He went on to elaborate, "I love the Father and do exactly what my Father has commanded me" (John 14:31).

But on the night of His arrest, being obedient to God's plan was torment. The fact that Jesus knew God's plan from the outset did not make it any easier to carry out. Jesus prayed, "If it is possible, may this cup be taken from me. Yet not my will, but yours" (Matthew 26:39). Knowing it was God's plan for the salvation of mankind, Jesus set aside His feelings and followed God's direction.

Obedience is carrying out the orders or plans of another. When the objective of the plan comports with our personal desires, obedience is easy. But obedience to godly authority often puts us to the test. Godly obedience may mean following a course of action that is different from our personal wants or desires—it is conducting ourselves in a fashion mandated by God. And that requires commitment.

You and I are called to be obedient to God's plan and to adhere to His principles—not just when it feels good, but also when it requires us to endure pain or make a personal sacrifice. We acknowledge as much when we pray, "thy will be done." (See Jesus' instruction in the Lord's Prayer, Matthew 6:10.)

God's will is expressed in His inspired words of scripture. God's will requires us to renew our mind, i.e., reorder our thinking (Romans 12:2). For example, being obedient to God's Word requires us to be faithful in our relationships, generous in our giving, and loving even toward our enemies (Matthew 5:27–48).

Obedience requires us to reject worldly thoughts and desires and substitute in its place a strong commitment to follow God, regardless of the cost. Jesus acknowledged that, "whoever does the will of my Father in heaven is my brother and sister..." (Matthew 12:50). And Paul directed that we are to "have the same mindset as Christ" (Philippians 2:5). Being Christian means that we strive to be obedient to God's standards for everyday living.

So consider these questions for introspection:

1. How are you learning what God's standards require?
2. When tempted to adhere to the ways of the world instead of God's principles, how do you find strength to remain true to your commitment to follow God?
3. Obedience is a learned behavior that sometimes means we have to correct our course. When you depart from God's standards, how do you get back on course?

Jesus set the example for us of what it means to be obedient. And since you and I are called to be obedient to God's standards, we must become familiar with scripture so that we are informed as to His standards for everyday living. Our commitment to godly living sometimes requires strength beyond our natural capability. Therefore, we must learn to follow the leading of God's Holy Spirit and team up with an accountability partner or a small group of Christian confidants who will strengthen and redirect us in love when we fall short.

Obedience is learned. It requires a conscious decision to follow Jesus' example, and it requires ongoing effort to obey—even when that is difficult. But obedience leads to freedom from Satan's domination and evidences us as children of God.

JESUS EATS WITH A TAX COLLECTOR

Matthew 9:10–17

Jesus stirred quite a controversy when he invited Matthew to become a disciple. Today's text, Matthew 9:9–13, is a first-person account—Matthew himself—explaining how it all happened.

As a starting point, it is important to understand who Matthew was. Matthew explains that he was sitting at his tax collector's booth when Jesus came along and simply said, "Follow me." Matthew says that he immediately got up and followed Jesus (Matthew 9:9). As a tax collector, Matthew was hated by his own people. He had been awarded the contract from the Roman government to collect tax payments from his fellow Jews. Matthew's compensation for this job was whatever extra money he could extract from his Jewish neighbors. And the Roman soldiers were there to enforce the tax assessments Matthew imposed.

Therefore, Matthew was considered a traitor to his own people. He was despised as someone who would prey upon his fellow Hebrews in order to advance his personal gain. In fact, as a tax collector Matthew would have been disqualified as a witness in court and would have been excommunicated from the synagogue.

And once Matthew left his tax-collector post to begin following the rabbi Jesus, he could never return to the lucrative position he'd been given by the Roman government. Nevertheless, he forfeited the occupation of taking from the people and became transformed to one who gave to others, followed Jesus, and eventually wrote one of the first handbooks about Jesus.

Jesus went to Matthew's home for dinner that evening, and that is where things became interesting. Matthew's dinner party included Jesus plus other tax collectors and a group of openly sinful people (Matthew 9:10). No self-respecting person would have stepped foot inside of the home of Matthew the tax collector. Yet Jesus ate and openly fraternized with notorious sinners. That relationship with sinners applies to you and me. Romans 5:8 instructs that "while we were yet sinners, Jesus died for our sake." Each of us have sinned and fallen short of God's standards (Romans 3:23).

The Pharisees gathered outside of Matthew's house and jeered at Jesus' disciples, "Why does your teacher eat with tax collectors and sinners?" (Matthew 9:11). The Pharisees were intimating that Jesus lacked piety and discernment.

Jesus had a ready answer. "It is not the healthy who need a doctor, but the sick." Jesus fully intended to be among sinners. That was the reason he had come to earth (1 Timothy 1:15 "Jesus came into the world to save sinners"). He came to heal the sin-sick soul. These were the very people he had come to save from the fires of hell. Conversely, the Pharisees were like doctors who wanted to avoid contact with sick people.

Then Jesus added a more esoteric challenge to the teachers of the law who were critical of Jesus' association with sinners, "go learn what is meant by 'I desire mercy, not sacrifice. For I have not come to call the righteous, but sinners'" (Matthew 9:13, Jesus quoting the prophet Hosea at Hosea 6:6).

The prophet Hosea was God's spokesman more than seven hundred years before the birth of Jesus. In Hosea 6:6 God—through his prophet—said that he "desired mercy, not sacrifice and acknowledgment of God rather than burnt offerings." Earlier in Old Testament times, God had instituted circumcision and animal sacrifice as a means of teaching obedience. But these rituals had become rote; they were performed as a near-meaningless gesture. Hosea instructed that God would much rather see heartfelt expressions like mercy for His people and respect for His standards for living. The Pharisees had become legalistic, choosing form over substance, ritual over pursuit of a true relationship with God.

Change was needed in the hearts of the people. Hope was absent, an endless stream of "dos and don'ts" reigning over everyday life. Those claiming to already be righteous were opposed to Jesus and would cling to their own ways. But those who knew they fell short of God's righteousness were open to Jesus and were susceptible to receive what he offered: a way to build a true relationship with God. Jesus suggested that the Jewish teachers needed to learn the real meaning of the message of the prophet Hosea.

Jesus risked his reputation, his social standing, and even his safety to stand by those who recognized that they needed a savior. And Matthew gave up his business and personal financial gain to promote the Kingdom of God. He became a bold and courageous spokesman.

What can we learn from Matthew's story? How does this scripture passage apply in our lives? Consider these questions for introspection:

1. Matthew forever walked away from a lucrative tax-collection business in order to follow Jesus. How are you following Jesus?
2. Matthew invited all his friends to come meet Jesus. Who are you inviting to meet Jesus?
3. Matthew partnered with Jesus to reach a world of sinners. How are you partnering with Jesus?

Jesus risked His earthly reputation by socializing with sinners and tax collectors—the people who were disdained by "proper" society. And Matthew gave up his profitable business, his home, and his luxurious lifestyle in order to become a disciple of Jesus.

For you and me, a life with Jesus is not about outward appearances of religious piety and pretense; rather, you and I are called to boldly partner with Jesus, working to reach a world of lost sinners, providing hope to the marginalized elements of society, and assuring them of God's love and desire for a personal and meaningful relationship. You and I are tasked with boldly making disciples of all nations.

JESUS' MISSION

Luke 4:14–21

Early in His ministry, Jesus visited his hometown synagogue in Nazareth. Jesus' popularity had been growing elsewhere in the region as a result of his wise teachings and his miraculous powers (Matthew 13:54). Initially, Jesus was well received at the synagogue in Nazareth, but the townspeople found it difficult to believe that Jesus could be anyone special. After all, Jesus had grown up in Nazareth; he was one of them.

Jesus sensed that the Nazareth crowd wanted proof. They needed to be "wowed" with miracles and healings like those reported from around the region. The undercurrent was "Do here in your hometown what we have heard that you did in Capernaum" (Luke 4:23). Jesus responded, "No prophet is accepted in his hometown" (Luke 4:24). Then Jesus reminded those gathered in the synagogue that God's presence was sometimes shown to foreigners and Gentiles because they had more faith in God than the Israelites.

Both Matthew and Mark report that Jesus "did not do many miracles there [in Nazareth] because of their lack of faith" (Matthew 13:58, Mark 6:5–6). But the Nazareth congregation took great offense at Jesus' suggestion that they lacked faith. Luke reports that the "people in the synagogue were furious when they heard this...they got up and drove Jesus out of town," hoping to throw him over a cliff (Luke 4:28–29).

But before the crowd turned hostile, Jesus used His visit to the Nazareth synagogue as an opportunity to announce His mission. On that particular Sabbath day, Jesus was handed the scroll of the prophet Isaiah from which to read. Jesus carefully unrolled the scripture to the particular place He had in mind. Then he read aloud from Isaiah 61:1–2. "The Spirit of the Lord is on me, because he has anointed me to proclaim the good news to the poor. He has sent me to proclaim freedom to the prisoners and recovery of sight to the blind, to set the oppressed free, to proclaim the year of the Lord's favor."

These were familiar words to the Jewish people. Nearly seven hundred years earlier, the prophet Isaiah had delivered these words to the Jewish exiles who had been driven from their homes in Israel. The exiles had lost their property, their health, and their hope at the hands of the cruel Assyrian armies.

The prophet Isaiah had spoken God's messages of judgment to the disobedient Jewish nation, but he also revealed God's plan for a savior. Isaiah foretold Christ's virgin birth (Isaiah 7:14), his proclamation of the good news (Isaiah 61:1), his sacrificial death (Isaiah 52:13–53:12), and his second coming (Isaiah 60:2–3).

As Jesus read from Isaiah's scroll, "the eyes of everyone in the synagogue were fastened on [Jesus]." (Luke 4:20).

Then He stopped, rolled up the scroll, and spoke words announcing His identity and mission. Jesus' words were these: "Today this scripture is fulfilled in your hearing" (Luke 4:21).

Although the Jewish congregation knew Isaiah's prophecy and yearned for the arrival of the Messiah, they were unable to accept him when he appeared.

Much like conditions at the time of Isaiah, the people in Jesus' time were mired in poverty brought on by the foreign forces that held them captive. And much like the people from Isaiah's era, the people were imprisoned by sin and were blinded to the true direction intended by God.

Isaiah had promised a time of jubilee, i.e., a time when debts would be cancelled, slaves freed, and relationships restored. But when the savior appeared before them, they were not prepared to recognize him. They missed the point that the Messiah's mission was spiritual in nature. He was cancelling sin debt and freeing people from enslavement to earthly strongholds and restoring their relationship with God.

Are we susceptible to the same doubts? Do we want Jesus to reveal Himself with miracles and extraordinary acts? Do our doubts cloud our understanding of the clear purpose of Jesus' ministry on earth? Are we able to think of Jesus' mission as one affecting our spiritual well-being?

Reflect with me, if you will, on these questions for introspection.

1. Jesus' mission was to proclaim good news
   to the poor. The good news was salvation

for the repentant sinner, i.e., one who was "poor in spirit" (see Matthew 5:3, the "poor in spirit" will inherit the kingdom of heaven). Are you coming into Jesus' presence acknowledging poverty or brokenness spiritually? How?

2. Jesus came to restore sight to the spiritually blind. Often, we are unable to see God's presence in our life because of a spiritual blind spot, such as a lack of forgiveness, unreleased anger, or lack of respect. What is your spiritual blind spot?

3. Jesus came to proclaim, "the year of the Lord's favor." There is power in speaking God's promises. What promises of God are you declaring?

The mission of Jesus is to restore relationships with God and to conquer sin so that it no longer can enslave God's people. Jesus healed, cast out demons, explained scripture, and taught about the Kingdom of God so that spiritual healing and restoration would occur. To receive the benefits of Jesus' ongoing mission, we need to resist the world's deceptive instruction that we need more physical proof, and we need to be open to His works within our spirit.

JESUS IS THE WORD OF GOD

John 1:1–18

Not long ago our son announced his engagement to a wonderful young lady. That word triggered an avalanche of planning and preparation in anticipation of the wedding event and life beyond that point. The word of their love has affected my life and my wife's life and the lives of many others. We eagerly read e-mails about their engagement and future plans. We are busy preparing for the wedding, making sure that we have everything in order so that we will be part of that blessed event. We have been drawn into a love story that is bigger than any one of us.

The Bible is much the same. The Bible is God's love letter to each of us. Through God's words of scripture, you and I are drawn into an everlasting love story—a story of God's love and its far-reaching effects. At the core of the Bible is word of the engagement of God's son, an announcement that directly affects us all because it is the announcement of our engagement—our engagement to the Son of

God. And this story is not just words in a book. God's son is very much alive.

The apostle John, inspired by God, wrote that God's Word, from the very beginning of time, demonstrated God's nature, reinforced His standards for living, and created the narrow path that leads to eternal life. Moreover, God's Word sprang to life and lived among us. More than inspired writings, God's Word became a living person. Jesus lived out God's standards and demonstrated His love. John wrote, "In the beginning was the Word and the Word was with God and the Word was God" (John 1:1). Then he added, "The Word became flesh and made His dwelling among us" (John 1:14).

The prophets of old wrote from God's inspiration. Isaiah, for example, wrote that "the Lord himself will give you a sign: The virgin will conceive and give birth to a son and you will call him Immanuel" (Isaiah 7:14). Seven hundred years later the Virgin Mary conceived by the work of the Holy Spirit and gave birth to a son who was called Immanuel, God with us (Matthew 1:18–23, Luke 1:27–31). God's Word was birthed to life—in Bethlehem—just as the prophet Micah had foretold. (Compare Micah 5:2 with Matthew 2:1 and Luke 2:4–6.)

God's ancient words spoke of a new covenant by which God would remember our sins no more. (Jeremiah 31:31–34). The prophet Isaiah elaborated that remission of our sins would be accomplished through one who would be "despised and rejected," "pierced for our transgressions," "cut off from the land of the living," as an "offering for sin" (Isaiah 55:3–10). Centuries later, just as God's Word had foretold, Jesus was led to the cross, as a sacrificial lamb, crucified for our sins (Matthew 26–27, Hebrews 9:15).

God's Word came to life and dwelt among us. His Holy Spirit remains within us (1 Corinthians 3:16). The prophecies of God's inspired Word have proven true. They have come to life. And the scriptures promise more to come. When Jesus returns to life on earth, He will take His church—His people—to be His bride (Revelation 19:7–9). Then Jesus will reign forever in the new Heaven and new earth—the restored Garden of Eden, once again coming to live on this world (Revelation 21:9–22:5, Psalm 2:6–9).

God, in the human form of Jesus, lived in the physical world so that you and I could have a better understanding of God and our spiritual home. The Bible's instructions came to life in the form of Jesus, providing the way for us to be joined with Christ in our eternal home (John 1:1–4, 14; 14:1–3). As we prepare for life with Jesus, reflect with me on these questions for introspection:

1. God's love letter, the Bible, tells of God's overwhelming love for us. What significance do you place on His love letter? How does the Bible's priority in your life compare with other priorities such as work, sports, family obligations, and material things?

2. Scripture announces our engagement to Jesus. What preparations are you making for this eternal partnership with Christ?

3. When He returns, everything will change in an instant—there will be no opportunity for last-minute adjustments. If His return occurred right now, what regrets would you have, i.e., what things would have been left undone?

The Words of scripture are a love story that came to life. And just as the Word became flesh and dwelt among us at the time of Jesus' ministry, the Word will once again return to earth in physical form, this time to inflict lasting judgment against evil and to gather up His bride, i.e., those who have given themselves to God's Son, Jesus. Preparation time is now. The wedding feast of the Lamb will soon be upon us. Come, Lord Jesus, come!

JESUS FORGIVES

2 Chronicles 7:14

For weeks now, the nonstop topic of conversation has been the coronavirus. But do you know that there is an even more prevalent and more deadly virus that has infected the entire population of the world? That virus is sin. Sin—rebellion and separation from God's plan—has infected every one of us, and the result of sin is death (Romans 6:23). But there is a vaccine: a gift from God that leads to eternal life—and that gift is Jesus Christ. (This remedy is listed in the second half of Romans 6:23.)

So how do we get ahold of this remedy? How do we receive the gift that counters the sin pandemic from which we all suffer? The key is found in the ancient scripture of 2 Chronicles 7:13–16. According to that passage, "When [God allows] a plague among [His] people" the prescription is as follows: "If my people, who are called by my name, will humble themselves and pray and seek my face and turn from their wicked ways, then I will hear from heaven, and I will forgive their sin and will heal their land."

While sickness and evil are not of God's making, He does sometimes use those conditions to turn the hearts of

His people back to Him. In those times, recovery begins with confession and repentance, i.e., seeking God's forgiveness. As Christians, you and I are people called by His name, the name of Christ. We are summoned to humbly acknowledge the sins in our land and to turn our face toward God and His plan for our lives. When we confess our sins openly and earnestly turn back to God, He promises forgiveness and healing.

Jesus forgives. He covered our sins. The cure for the sin virus is available to all who will accept Jesus' sacrifice and turn their ways toward Him. Scripture promises, "If you declare with your mouth, 'Jesus is Lord,' and believe in your heart that God raised Him from the dead, you will be saved" (Romans 10:9).

King Solomon counseled that God's mercy follows for those who openly confess and renounce their sin (Proverbs 28:13). Often, we think of forgiveness on a personal level. Jesus died for our sins (John 3:16). We ask for personal forgiveness, as we forgive one another. (Matthew 6:12). Forgiveness is available over and over (Matthew 18:22).

But forgiveness also has a corporate aspect to it. God instructed Moses about standards for nations; a nation following godly principles would be blessed, and a nation that drifts away from God would suffer curses (Deuteronomy 28). God also instructed that when a nation returned to God, after having strayed and repented, "then the Lord will restore [the nation's] fortunes" (Deuteronomy 30:3).

History notes that when George Washington took the oath as president of the United States, he opened his Bible to Deuteronomy 28 before placing his hand on the Bible for the administration of the oath of office. By doing so, Washington was claiming God's promises of national blessings as this country worked to follow God's mandates. That same scripture promised curses should the nation abandon God's ways.

Early in the history of this nation, biblical principles undergirded government and laws. Congress used tax dollars to print Bibles for use as readers in public schools. Prayer began every school day and every government meeting. Religion was respected, and human life was recognized as being the image of God.

To be sure, our nation had its downfalls, but the overall direction was to recognize and respect God's role in the life of the nation. During those early years our nation was blessed. Our borders were secure, our food sources were bountiful, and our military succeeded against despots and tyrants around the world. The fledgling nation was blessed.

As time passed, however, God was eliminated from public schools, government meetings, and social functions. Even symbols like the cross or the Ten Commandments came under attack. Human life was no longer respected; baby killing was not only tolerated but was given constitutional protection, resulting in the killing of more than sixty million unborn infants offered to the false god of "reproductive rights."

And here we are today. The World Trade Centers are gone, and our borders have become porous. A worldwide pandemic is killing people, destroying businesses, disrupting trade, and exacerbating natural disasters—such as hurricanes, earthquakes, wildfires, and global warming—all of which are prevalent at levels never before known.

Does this sound like a time when we, as a nation, as a congregation, and as a Christian people need to humble ourselves and pray, acknowledging our corporate wrongdoing and correcting the course of our nation—our church—our community of faith? You bet!

The plagues that oppress us today just might be God's way of turning this wayward nation back to Him. Now, more than ever, we need to remember that Jesus forgives. When we humble ourselves in prayer, confessing the sins of our nation and turning our direction back to God, Jesus—the Jesus who died in payment of our sins—will hear our pleas, forgive our sins, and heal our land.

Jesus is the great healer. We, as a nation, need His healing. Scripture provides the formula. So reflect with me, if you will, on these questions for introspection:

1. We are in a time of national malaise. The symptoms are seen in the health pandemic, growing natural disasters, and gridlock in government that affect us as a nation. How has this nation drifted away from God, and what are you doing about it?

2. National revival can bring about national healing. Revival begins with each of us. What steps are you taking to advance the cause for returning this nation to God?

3. Although the symptoms are physical, the battle we face is spiritual (Ephesians 6:12). The weapon we've been issued is "the sword of the Spirit which is the Word of God." How are you using the Word of God—His inspired scripture—in this time of war?

Forgiveness is there for the asking—for us personally and for our nation. Jesus died for our sins. He is the key to forgiveness and healing. When sinful ways have become the way of the nation, scripture promises curses for that nation—curses that will drive the nation to its knees in prayer and repentance. Join the national effort to make America one nation under God once again. Join the prayers of repentance for our nation.

JESUS PROMISES
THE HOLY SPIRIT
John 14:1–14

D o you ever feel like you are being whipsawed between the forces of this world and God's spiritual direction for your life? That's not an illusion. You and I are the objects of a spiritual tug of war—a battle for eternal placement of our souls. Scripture alludes to that battle in Jude 9 where Satan fights with the archangel Michael over the remains of God's servant, Moses.

Satan's goal is to permanently separate souls from the presence of God. In this physical world, Satan has been allowed temporary dominion (1 John 5:19). Left unchecked, Satan inflicts indiscriminate destruction of our physical bodies and resources, as well as our souls. The current pandemic, COVID-19, likely is an example. Satan sows doubt, anger, fear, confusion, pain, turmoil, and disruption in an effort to distract people away from their Maker (See 1 Peter 5:8).

But Jesus has counseled us to stand strong, knowing that Satan and his minions can destroy the body but not the soul (Matthew 10:28). And while the body eventually returns to dust, the spirit God breathed into mankind's soul returns to God (Ecclesiastes 12:7) for His final judgment (Revelation 20:11–15).

Jesus came to earth to be on the front lines, experiencing firsthand the tactics employed by Satan in his effort to perpetually separate mankind from God. Jesus intimated as much when He explained, "I will ask the Father and He will give you another advocate—the Spirit of Truth" (John 14:16–17). That Spirit of Truth—God's Holy Spirit—employs God's inspired Words to provide a sword for our use in the ongoing battle for our soul (Ephesians 6:17).

The Holy Spirit assists us in the daily battle, and Jesus provides the ultimate cover for our sins so that we can remain in the presence of our Maker forever. Both are available for those who accept Jesus as Lord of their life and who heed the leading of the Holy Spirit. Availing ourselves of the cover—the blood sacrifice of Jesus—and directions sent by God's Holy Spirit requires our conscious decision.

Scripture makes clear that the war for our souls is a battle of spiritual dimensions (Ephesians 6:12). Jesus promised the Holy Spirit as our commander in the everyday skirmishes and in the full-blown wars over the destiny for our souls; God's Spirit is embedded within us (John 14:17). Our bodies house the Holy Spirit; we are God's temples (1 Corinthians 6:19).

Even before His departure, Jesus provided a foretaste of God's Holy Spirit for His disciples (John 20:22). And shortly before His ascension into Heaven, Jesus advised His followers of the great power vested in the Holy Spirit that they were about to receive (Acts 1:8). And when God's promised Spirit arrived with the force of wind and fire, God's followers were blown away by the healings, the wisdom, the guidance, and the conversions that resulted. (See Acts 2.)

That same power—the power that raised Jesus from the dead—is available to you and me (Romans 8:11). Just as Jesus promised, the Holy Spirit's power was sent for our guidance and empowerment. Amazingly, however, some people reject the Holy Spirit; they ignore the Word of God that is the sword of the Spirit, opting instead to follow distortions from the devil that appeal to their self-centered motives.

The job of the Holy Spirit is to direct our thoughts, words, and deeds back to Jesus. What would Jesus do or say or think in these circumstances? Too often, when the Holy Spirit gently speaks, our reaction is to resist His leading. God's Word, after all, is sometimes difficult to follow. Satan suggests that openly making disciples is not socially correct, or God certainly did not say that sexual immorality was wrong, or God could not have meant what He said in scripture.

Because we have been endowed with free choice, we can disregard the Holy Spirit and the Word of God. We have the personal power to be insensitive to His leading in our life. Repeated resistance against the Holy Spirit's guidance eventually creates spiritual calluses—a condition that scripture calls hardening of the heart.

In his letter to the early church in Ephesus, Paul explained that those who suffered "futility in their thinking," i.e., had "lost all sensitivity" to the leading of the Holy Spirit were, as a result, suffering from hardening of their hearts (Ephesians 4:17–19). Jesus referenced Isaiah's prophecy that those who resisted God's direction had hearts that had become calloused and therefore were no longer able to hear God's leading. (See Matthew 13:15, where Jesus quoted from Isaiah 6:9–10.)

King Solomon's wisdom includes this passage: "Blessed is the one who always trembles before God, but whoever hardens their heart falls into trouble" (Proverbs 28:14). When our heart remains open to God's leading by His Holy Spirit, blessings follow. But woe to the one who constantly resists God's leading. Eventually his heart will be hardened to the Word of God.

Jesus promised the Holy Spirit as our everyday— every moment—spiritual advisor. When He made that promise, He noted that those who follow the ways of the world would not accept the Holy Spirit's leading, but His followers would have a guide for godly living even after Jesus returned to Heaven (John 14:16–18). So, reflect for a moment if you will on these questions for introspection:

1. James, the half-brother of Jesus advised that Spiritual wisdom—the wisdom promised by Jesus in the form of the Holy Spirit—is available for the asking (James 1:5). How are you seeking the leading of Holy Spirit in your life?
2. God is Spirit (John 4:24), and you and I are made in His image (Genesis 1:27).

Moreover, our spirit returns to God after our earthly body is depleted (Ecclesiastes 12:7). How are you feeding your spirit?

3. We are cautioned not to harden our hearts (Hebrews 3:8). But if we remain insensitive to His leading, eventually our hearts become callused, hardened against the influence of the Holy Spirit. Fortunately, the Word of God is sharper than a two-edged sword and is able to cut through the calluses and pierce our very essence (Hebrews 4:12). How are you remaining in the Word each day?

Jesus knew what He was doing when He asked the Father to provide His Holy Spirit as a living guide and counselor for mankind. That Spirit is a powerful and important gift—too significant to be ignored because it is the tool Jesus provided for our engaging in the everyday spiritual battles of life.

Don't quench the Spirit (1 Thessalonians 5:19); neither become insensitive to the leading of the Holy Spirit because, over time, that can cause our hearts to harden against the ways of our Lord. Embrace the Holy Spirit. He is a gift from God in Heaven.

JESUS EQUIPS US

Matthew 28:16–20

On December 22, 1885, a violent storm swept over an ocean region known as the graveyard of the Atlantic. Captain Patrick Etheridge, keeper of the Cape Hatteras light, noticed a ship that had blown onto Diamond Shoals and was being pounded into pieces. Captain Etheridge summoned his team at the lifesaving station to launch a rescue of the souls aboard the doomed ship. He issued the order to go—go to the rescue. Legend has it that a young novitiate at the lifesaving station questioned the captain's command, "But if we go, we may never make it back." Etheridge, keeping an eye on the disaster unfolding before him, elaborated, "We are required to go. We are not required to return."

One of the last commands given by Jesus before ending His in-person ministry on earth was to "go." Go make disciples of all nations—that is go even beyond our comfort zone. Go, reach souls in distress wherever they may be found and lead them to safety in Jesus. The Great Commission in Matthew 28:16–20, is Jesus' command for us to go.

Often, we resist the command. We wonder, what if we are changed in the process? What if we don't make it back to our current comfortable station in life? But the command is to "go." And sometimes that does not allow us to return to who we were before we responded to the command.

Jesus has commissioned each of us to be His ambassadors, rescuers spreading the Good News that Jesus has covered our sins so that we can enter the narrow portal that leads to eternal life. He does not want anyone to perish but wants everyone to come to repentance and eternal life (2 Peter 3:9). Moreover, He has promised to be with us every step of the way (Matthew 28:20).

And if He calls us, we can be assured that he will equip us, making certain that we have the provisions needed for the mission. In Paul's letter to the church at Philippi Paul assured Christ's followers that God would meet all their needs as they worked to advance the Kingdom of God (Philippians 4:19). And God is able to do immeasurably more than all we can ask or even imagine (Ephesians 3:20). The writer of Hebrews knew that God would equip His people with every good thing required for doing the will of God. (Hebrews 13:21). "God is able to bless abundantly, so that in all things at all times, having all that you need, you will abound in every good work (2 Corinthians 9:8).

So you might be thinking, *Okay, God, go ahead and equip me, then I'll move forward with your call to make disciples of all nations.* But typically, that's not the way it works. We need to move forward in faith, knowing that God is sending provisions to the place to which we've been called.

The prophet Elijah demonstrated this truth in 1 Kings chapter 17. God gave Elijah a command to go. Elijah went and God made provision for Elijah as he moved out in compliance with God's directive. As Elijah traveled, he received food from ravens and drank water from the brook. Again, he was told to "go." Provisions were made for Elijah at the appointed destination. Elijah received sustenance from a widow and she, in turn, received provision as she began to follow God's direction. In each instance, needs were met after moving forward in obedience to God's command.

When a football quarterback makes a pass, he throws the ball not to the present location of the receiver; instead, the ball is thrown to the receiver's intended destination. Likewise, God sends provisions ahead to the place and circumstances to which we are called, requiring us to first move out in faith, complying with God's command, knowing that God is sending His provisions.

We can be certain of these three things: (1) we are called to go make disciples of all nations, (2) God will make provisions for His will to be accomplished, and (3) the provisions are sent ahead for us after we move forward under God's direction. So consider these questions for introspection:

1. What is God calling you to do?
2. How are you stepping out in faith to advance the message of salvation through Jesus?
3. What provision do you need in order to disciple someone else in principles for Christian living?

The point of the Great Commission is that we are to go—to venture out, spreading the Gospel message. We can go with assurance that Jesus is with us always. Jesus will provide the opportunities, the words, and the resources needed for us to spread Jesus' directives for godly living. And we receive those provisions once we first venture out in faith.

So let's answer the call to go make disciples of all nations, baptizing and teaching in the name of Jesus, with the confidence that Christ is with us and that He will provide for our needs as we move out in faith.

JESUS SENDS ME
Matthew 9:35–10:8

The coronavirus pandemic disrupted food processing in the United States, resulting in vast fields of mature crops being plowed under and herds of cattle and hogs being wasted. The potential harvest was plentiful, but the workers were few, resulting in hungry people starving in the midst of plentiful food sources.

Jesus observed similar conditions—on a spiritual level—as He walked through the villages and countryside during His ministry. Although He worked tirelessly, healing and teaching wherever He went, He simply could not reach every soul. In Matthew's account, Jesus felt compassion for the people He saw; they were "harassed and helpless, like sheep without a shepherd" (Matthew 9:36). Jesus turned to His disciples and said, "The harvest is plentiful, but the workers are few. Ask the Lord of the harvest to send out workers into His field" (Matthew 9:37–38).

Jesus saw the unreached masses and was aware of many others who populated the world and would not have the opportunity to encounter Jesus. Even with His band of disciples, souls would be lost—never reached even though they were in desperate need. Jesus did not want to lose even a single person (John 6:39, 2 Peter 3:9). More workers were needed to feed the spiritually hungry of the world.

So Jesus deputized His disciples to work on His behalf. He "gave them authority to drive out impure spirits and to heal every disease and sickness" (Matthew 10:1). He prioritized their work: "Go...to the lost sheep of Israel" and not yet to the Gentiles or even the Samaritans (Matthew 10:5–6). Later, the apostle Paul recognized that the Gospel message went first to the Jews because of God's special and long-standing relationship with the Hebrew nation, but then was to be spread to the rest of the world (Romans 1:16).

When Jesus authorized His disciples to go out on Jesus' behalf to reach the people, He gave his representatives specific instructions and the power to accomplish them. "As you go, proclaim this message," Jesus directed, "The Kingdom of Heaven has come near" (Matthew 10:7). Heaven, of course, is that spiritual kingdom where God reigns. Jesus was all about doing God's will (John 14:10). He even taught His disciples to pray that God's will be done on earth, just as it is done in Heaven (Matthew 6:10). Heaven enters the earth plane whenever God's will is being done.

And Jesus provided His disciples with the power of the Holy Spirit to enable them to execute God's will of healing and driving out Satan's influence (Matthew 10:1, John 20:22).

As Jesus was about to leave earth, physically, He expanded the mission of His representatives. "Go make disciples of all nations," He ordered (Matthew 28:18–20). Just as the scope of the mission to spread the Gospel message was increased, so were the work force and the dispensation of power. Jesus has deputized all believers to be His ambassadors (2 Corinthians 5:20). We are called to be a priestly people, telling others about God's plan for salvation (1 Peter 2:9).

And Jesus has empowered us to do His work on earth—that is announcing the presence of God and healing in the name of Jesus. The Holy Spirit, promised by Jesus (John 14:16), holds great power (Acts 1:8, Romans 8:11). God's Holy Spirit presence lives within the hearts of believers (1 Corinthians 3:16). We are called to call upon that Holy Spirit power as we advance the Kingdom of Heaven, in the name of Jesus. (See John 14:13).

If we've been appointed to be the representatives of Jesus on earth, and if we've been empowered by the indwelling Holy Spirit to lead souls to Christ and to heal all sickness and disease, then why aren't we seeing massive healings and revival? Even Jesus' disciples encountered difficulty as the representatives of God's Kingdom. In Matthew 17:14–18, a desperate father came to Jesus begging for healing for his son. The father reported, "I brought him to your disciples but they could not heal him." Jesus healed the boy and later explained to His disciples that their attempts to heal the boy were prevented by the disciples' lack of faith.

Faith and the Holy Spirit work hand in hand. The Holy Spirit takes up residence in the souls of believers (1 Corinthians 3:16), but making use of God's Spirit power requires faith. Faith is "confidence in what we hope for and assurance about what we do not see" (Hebrews 11:1).

The people of our day are wandering aimlessly seeking spiritual direction. Satan has a foothold and is leading masses on a path of moral decay and rejection of godly order. The potential harvest of souls is great but the workers for God's Kingdom are few. You and I are the answer to Jesus' prayer for additional workers in the field.

Consider these questions, if you will, for introspection:

1. Where do you see the greatest need for God's healing and influence today? (God may be calling that need to your attention.)
2. The Great Commission is to "go." How are you "going" out and teaching, preaching, and baptizing, leading people to Christ's path for life?
3. When you accept Christ as your Savior, Holy Spirit takes up residence within you, providing a storehouse of power to be released in the exercise of faith in Jesus. What steps are you taking to bolster your faith?

The observation that Jesus made more than two thousand years ago still rings true today. The potential harvest of souls is great—overwhelming—and the workers in the field are few. That's why you, and I have been recruited—through the Great Commission—to work in the field for God's Kingdom. We are called to set the example for

Christian living and to not give Satan a foothold in our communities (Ephesians 4:25–32). Answer the call to work in the fields of human souls. The harvest is plentiful, but the workers are few.

JESUS CALMS THE STORMS

Matthew 8:23–27

I'd like to offer a challenge to men everywhere. This is the challenge: be spiritual leaders in your household and in your communities.

We live in tumultuous times. Storms are raging in our lives. We are suffering the effects of the coronavirus pandemic; we are living in economic collapse—worldwide, rioting and looting have scarred our cities; chasms of deep division along racial lines and socioeconomic lines splinter our world. And as if the real-life problems were not bad enough, our media (radio, TV, print, and Internet outlets) insist on taking sides, promoting one political extreme or another as the solution to our woes.

But the source of our troubles is not of this world. "Our struggle is not against flesh and blood, but against the rulers, against the authorities, against the powers of this dark world and against the spiritual forces of evil in the heavenly realms." Scripture says so at Ephesians 6:12. And there is not a political solution for our spiritual problem. There is not an economic solution for our spiritual problem. There is not a racial or nationality solution for our spiritual problem.

Men, we need to put on our "big boy" pants—our spiritual armor—and lead. We need to be sensitive to the needs of our children (Ephesians 6:4 instructs us to not exasperate our children). We need to be spiritual leaders in our families—leading and loving sacrificially as Christ did for His church (Ephesians 5:25). And we need to set the example of living in humility. Did you know that all contention in our lives begins with pride? (In Proverbs 13:10 we read, "Only pride causes contention.")

Matthew 8:23–27 tells the story of Jesus calming the sea as He and His disciples were rowing into a storm on their way to Gadarenes. Jesus exercised His spiritual powers to calm the wind and waves. At Gadarenes they encountered demon-possessed men. Scripture tells us that the spiritual demons were so violent there that they blocked progress for anyone seeking to go through that region (Matthew 8:28). Jesus, employing God's power, drove the demons away.

You and I, as believers, house the same Holy Spirit that Jesus used to overcome spiritual storms and difficulties (1 Corinthians 3:16, Romans 8:11). And men, we are called to be the Spirit leaders in our homes and in our communities, listening for God's direction and exercising the power of the Holy Spirit as Jesus did.

The storms we encounter in this world are the product of spiritual forces of wickedness. As men, we have been charged with the direction to lead, and equipped with the armor of God, and the implement for spiritual battle—the sword of scripture (Ephesians 6:11–17).

This year, I challenge all men to be spiritual leaders and for us to honor our Fathers who have gone before us. The commandment to honor our Fathers (and Mothers) "is the first [of the Ten Commandments] with a promise"—honor them "so that it may go well with you and that you may enjoy life on earth" (Ephesians 6:2–3, quoting from Exodus 20:12). Honor is due our fathers who have led (as best they knew how) their families and communities through the everyday spiritual battlefields. Through spiritual leadership we get to enjoy our God-given life on earth.

So reflect, if you will, on these questions for introspection:

1. How are you honoring the men who have mentored you?
2. How are you shouldering the responsibility as a point man to protect others as they encounter the storms of life at a spiritual level?
3. Exercising Holy Spirit power requires faith (see Matthew 17:20). What steps are you taking to develop your faith?

Storms are a fact of life on earth at the present time. The source of our storms is spiritual. Jesus has provided us with the tools and the direction to power through the storms by lifting every situation to God in prayer. By meeting storms with spiritual petitions, we are promised the "peace of God which transcends all understanding" (Philippians 4:6–7).

May we honor the men who have led us through hard times, and may we who are men step up our game to be the spiritual leaders that are so greatly needed at this time in the world.

JESUS HEALS US

John 9:1–12

Healing was a significant part of Jesus' ministry, one of the signs and wonders directing people to Jesus' identity as Messiah. Scripture shows that He never turned down a request for healing. (In Matthew 4:23, Jesus was "healing every disease and sickness among the people"; and Luke 6:19 "healing them all"; and Mark 6:56, "And wherever he went…all who touched [Him] were healed.") Later, when Jesus promised the power of the Holy Spirit, He told His disciples, "whoever believes in me will do the works I have been doing…ask in my name and I will do it" (John 14:12–14).

We know, therefore, that Jesus has the will and the ability to heal. Moreover, He has sent the healing power of the Holy Spirit into the hearts of believers (Acts 1:8; 2). Today we read about miraculous healings that have been done in the name of Jesus—not just at the time of Jesus, but also in today's world. Books have been written on the topic and prayer warriors are at work this very moment, praying for healings.

Yet some healings that are sought seem never to take place. Scripture suggests that some healings can be blocked by doubt or unreleased guilt or pent-up unforgiveness. (See, e.g., 1 John 1:9, Hosea 4:6, Hebrews 11:6, Matthew 21:21.) But frankly we don't fully understand why some healings are done in this lifetime and others not. This is one of those areas where we see dimly as through a darkened glass (as Paul wrote in 1 Corinthians 13:12). Sometimes intervention is required by others in the form of intercessory prayer. (See, e.g., Matthew 17:21.) But all healings are for the glory of God and are to be used to bring people to Him (John 9:3).

We know that sin has entered this world, bringing with it pain and sickness (Genesis 3:17–19). But when Jesus came, He repeatedly exclaimed, "The kingdom of God is near." In the kingdom of God—which is Heaven—there is no pain, illness, or suffering. (Revelation 21:4 promises that when Heaven and Earth are reformed and joined, "there will be no more death or mourning or crying or pain, for the old order of things has passed away.")

When the miraculous heavenly power of God's Spirit intervenes, healing is accomplished. Scripture confirms that healing is God's intent. When we don't see the healing we seek in this lifetime, we can be assured that the healings are nevertheless accomplished in the next life.

Current day stories of near-death experiences often include reports of seeing once crippled people, running freely, healed of their affliction, or stillborn infants who are thriving in perfect life in Heaven. We can be confident that healings that we expect but do not see during our lifetime occur in the next life. Prayers do not return void. (Isaiah 55:11). Rest assured that even prayers for healing that seem unanswered are in fact heard and healings take place—just not always in the time or method that we contemplate. But then God's thoughts are not our thoughts, His ways are not our ways (Isaiah 55:8).

You and I are spiritual beings, made in God's image and God is Spirit (John 4:24). We are temporarily housed in earth suits; our bodies serve as covers for our Spiritual self while we are on earth (2 Corinthians 5:1). Lasting healings take place in the Spirit. Nevertheless, we are encouraged to ask for repair of even the temporary body housing our Spirit.

Isaiah 53:5 is often quoted when healing is discussed. That passage says, "by His wounds we are healed." That healing comes by virtue of Jesus' suffering in our place, paying our sin debt and freeing us from the eternal pain of separation from God. That's explained in 1 Peter 2:24: Jesus "bore our sins in His body on the cross, so that we might die to sin and live for righteousness—by His wounds you have been healed." Likewise, Paul pointed out that "in Christ all will be made alive" (1 Corinthians 15:22).

Healing is assured in eternal life. But when Jesus ministered in person, on earth, He was able to dispense healings of earthly bodies, and He made provision for that healing ministry to be carried on even after He returned to Heaven. Earthly healings take place when Heaven's power reaches into this world—when God's will is done on earth as it is in Heaven. (A familiar line from the Lord's Prayer, Matthew 6:10.)

When God's Holy Spirit entered the hearts of people on earth, that healing power was made available to us. That's why James, the brother of Jesus wrote, "Is anyone among you sick? Let them call the elders of the church to pray over them with oil in the name of the Lord. And the prayer offered in faith will make the sick person well; the Lord will raise them up. If they have sinned, they will be forgiven" (James 5:13–15). He also instructed, "Therefore confess your sins to each other and pray for each other so that you may be healed. The prayer of a righteous person is powerful and effective" (James 5:6).

Jesus heals us. When that healing takes place in our temporary earth bodies, the forces of Heaven have intervened. Jesus taught that we should boldly and persistently declare God's healing for illness and pain suffered on earth. We can be assured that God hears our prayers and answers them. God does not favor disease or pain.

So reflect with me, if you will, on a few questions for introspection:

1. Do you believe that the power of the Holy Spirit that dwells in believers includes the power of healing? Why? Or Why not?
2. Scripture instructs us to pray for those who are sick or injured. Are you praying for healing for someone or are you leaving that up to others?
3. When the healing you seek does not appear, how do you reconcile that with Jesus' example and teachings?

The power of the Holy Spirit to heal has long been discussed but is frequently a mystery. Scripture is clear on at least some aspects of healing: Jesus heals us, Jesus favors healing, and we are to persistently and expectantly pray for healing. When healing has not occurred it is appropriate to ask, is something blocking healing such as unrepented sin or lack of forgiveness or overwhelming doubt? But the purpose of asking those questions is never to add guilt or shame to the injured or ill person. These are questions for self-inspection.

And when healing eludes us, recognize that by His stripes (i.e., the suffering of Jesus when He paid for our sins) we are healed. That healing may take place on earth, but it surely takes place in Heaven. Praise God that illness and pain are never permanent for those who accept Jesus as savior because He has already healed us.

JESUS FREES US
Romans 8:1–8; Matthew 9:20–22

Imagine being convicted for an offense and sentenced to prison, but then being declared innocent and set free. Rarely is such relief granted under the law. In fact, being set free from a conviction requires granting of an extraordinary writ known as a writ of actual innocence. Writs of actual innocence are seldom granted.

You and I are natural-born sinners, and the penalty for sin is death (Romans 6:23). We are guilty of breaking God's standards in our thoughts, words, and deeds. Sin's contamination throughout the world has brought on widespread sickness, addiction, and pain. But Jesus covers the sins of all who declare Him as their savior (Romans 10:9). By paying our sin debt, He has released us from death row, a writ of innocence has issued, and we are set free from eternal bondage, pain and death caused by our sin. (Romans 8:1–2 instructs that "there is no condemnation for those who are in Christ Jesus...we have been set free.") Sometimes earthly consequences remain, but we've been set free from the eternal effects of our sins.

We are blessed in this country to be able to openly confess Jesus as our savior. The constitutional guarantee of freedom to exercise our faith removes legal barriers for Christians in this country. We are free to openly call on the name of Jesus and to share His Gospel message. That freedom to exercise our faith allows us to celebrate being released from the effects of sin.

Even in the midst of trying times, we can receive peace that transcends human understanding (Philippians 4:7). We can be healed of conditions that separate us in relationships with one another (Matthew 9:20). We can be freed from anxieties and pain because we live with the assurance that Jesus is with us always and that He has covered the eternal penalty for our sins (Matthew 28:20, Romans 10:9). We can be freed from crippling worry because our perspective is that of citizens of Heaven (Matthew 6:33). We can be freed from lasting effects of sin because the Spirit that raised Jesus from the dead is now embedded in the hearts of believers (Romans 8:11, 1 Corinthians 3:16).

We live in the land of the free, and as a result we can openly praise Jesus for His freeing grace—for His having released us from the penalties due us for our sinful nature.

In recent years many have debated whether this country was founded on Christian principles. Beliefs of the Founding Fathers have been analyzed, and their references to scripture have been explained away by some as simply a reflection of the culture of that time. But if we go to the very earliest of European settlers venturing into the New World, there is no doubt: this land was dedicated to Jesus.

And likewise, there can be no doubt that a place committed to Jesus is a place where freedom can reign.

In the early 1600s, an Anglican priest named Richard Hakluyt labored to convince Britain's Queen to support a mission to the New World. A promotional pamphlet from that effort stated that the primary purpose of the venture would be to plant religion. Shortly after King James came to the throne, he authorized the charter for the Virginia Company of London—a charter that promoted "propagating of Christian religion" in the New World.

By the time that the company left Great Britain, Hakluyt was too old for the trip, so he was replaced by a younger Anglican priest, Robert Hunt, as chaplain for the group. After five harrowing months at sea, the company finally reached the shores of Cape Henry—in present-day Virginia Beach, Virginia. Upon their arrival Hunt required the group to remain on board their ship for another three days of prayer before disembarking.

And once the members of the Virginia Company stepped onto the beach, they immediately posted an oak cross. More prayers were lifted during which Chaplain Hunt declared, "From these very shores the Gospel shall go forth to not only the New World, but to the entire world." Following that dedication of this land to the promotion of God's purpose, the members of the Virginia Company returned to their ship and continued inland, up the James River, posting wooden crosses as they stopped on the shores along the way.

From the very outset of efforts to colonize this land, the purpose has been clear: this land is to be the base of operations for promoting the freeing grace of Jesus Christ. This is the land of the free—a place where we are free to exercise our faith in Jesus and therefore a place where we can receive and share the freeing grace of our Lord who died to bring about our freedom from bondage.

We are blessed to be able to openly celebrate our freedom—a freedom resulting from Jesus giving His earthly life for us and a freedom guaranteed by those who have laid down their life for the sake of this land.

As recipients of the freeing grace—the unearned blessings—given by Jesus, let's consider these questions for introspection:

1. From what has Jesus freed you?
2. As we celebrate our freedoms, how are you expressing thanksgiving to Jesus for His sacrifice made for our freedoms?
3. What steps are you taking to help preserve this as the land of the free—a land where we are free to openly receive and share the freeing grace of Jesus?

As we celebrate living in the land of the free, let's also be mindful of what that means for our relationship with Jesus. He suffered death on the cross in order to free you and me from the permanent effects of our sin. Once we accept Jesus as Lord over our life, there is no condemnation because Jesus has freed us from the law of sin and death (Romans 8:2).

Because of the sacrifice made by Jesus, we can be healed from the eternal bondage that is brought on by sin; we can be freed of pains, addictions, and snares that otherwise would separate us eternally from our Maker. We live in the land of the free where we can openly promote the freeing grace that Jesus established by dying on the cross for our sake.

Praise Jesus!

JESUS SOWS SEEDS

Matthew 13:1–23

I meet with an accountability group each week. Our purpose is to encourage one another to grow in our faith walk. We start each session with the same question: where are you seeing God at work in your life? For disciples of Jesus, that should be an easy question. After all, the Kingdom of God is near, and the Holy Spirit is constantly at work in our midst. But surprisingly, we are often hard pressed to identify God at work in our life.

The world around us provides an overload of stimuli: sights and sounds of pandemics, marches, violence, division, jobs or the absence of jobs (the list is endless). These things overload our senses, blinding us to God's work that is being carried out in our midst.

Jesus often spoke in parables. His disciples asked Him why. Jesus explained that he spoke in parables, knowing that some would get it, and others would not (Matthew 13:13–17). The prophets, He explained, foretold this human condition. Jeremiah wrote, "You foolish and senseless people, who have eyes but do not see [and] who have ears but do not hear" (Jeremiah 5:21). Similarly, Isaiah warned that those whose hearts had become calloused by resisting God's directives would be "ever hearing, but never understanding [and] ever seeing but never perceiving" (Isaiah 6:9–10).

In Matthew 13:1–23, Jesus told the parable of the four soils. "A farmer went out to sow seed," He explained. But not all the seed grew into crops. Some of the seed was snatched up and eaten by the birds. Jesus later explained that the birds in the story represented "the evil one [who] comes and snatches away what is sown in the hearts of [mankind]" (Matthew 13:19). He continued in the parable, saying that some of the seed fell on rocky places lacking good soil. This, He explained, represented the Word of God that was initially accepted by people, but whose faith withered and died because they never developed a root system of understanding to support the seed that had been planted (Matthew 13:21).

Still, other seed was choked out by weeds and thorns. This, Jesus explained, represented those who received His word but focused instead on the worries and troubles of this world and that overshadowed their faith (Matthew 13:22).

But the farmer's seed that fell on good soil—conditions receptive to growth—produced an abundant crop. This category represented those persons who heard the Word of God and were receptive to its influence in their lives (Matthew 13:23).

The seed in Jesus' story was God's inspired word. God's Word became flesh and dwelt among us in the form of Jesus (John 1:14). You and I are the medium—the soil in which the seed (the Word of God)—can grow. Are we receptive to scripture? Or does Satan snatch that influence away from us, or are we so caught up in the stimuli of the day that we're unable to focus on scripture and let it grow in our soul?

The truth, likely, is that each of us is represented by each of the soil types. Sometimes we take the time to retreat from the busyness of the day, so that we can meditate on God's inspired words of scripture. On those occasions we read from the Bible, then we pray about what we've read, we ponder how those words apply in our life, and we grow in spiritual insight.

But at other times, we yield to the pagan influences of this world, ignoring God's Word and viewing it as "politically incorrect" or narrow-minded or judgmental. Sometimes we mean well: we listen to a sermon or scripture reading but never find the time to follow up for in depth growth. Our scriptural root system remains shallow and susceptible to being wiped out in a crisis. And still other times we earnestly work at building a strong relationship with God's Word only to be overcome by the realities of everyday life: time pressures, worries about work, family, and relationships.

The seed—God's Word—is constantly being broad-cast. Sometimes it falls on a receptive heart, and sometimes it does not. Sometimes we have the ears and eyes to perceive God at work in our presence, and sometimes we are oblivious. What makes the difference?

In the world of agriculture, farmers prepare the soil for planting in order to enhance the likelihood of a successful crop. Preparing the ground to make it receptive to the seed requires planning and dedication. Fields are plowed and harrowed, fertilized and placed in orderly rows. Great time and expense are spent simply to get the soil ready to receive the seed.

Likewise, you and I need to consciously decide to be receptive to the seed of God's Word. We need to set aside time without worldly distractions so that we can prayerfully meditate on God's Word. We need to view the world from God's perspective. Look for Him—He's here beside us, walking through the challenges of life with us.

Rather than being blinded by tragedy or the lunacy around us, can we pause and ask God for wisdom (see James 1:5)? Can we find His message—"return to Me"—buried in Satan's pandemic or divisions? If we will take the time and the effort to prepare our hearts to receive God's Word, we will see Him in our midst.

Seeing God at work and hearing His message in the everyday cacophony is not a passive exercise. When we resolve to find God and hear Him, and when we consciously commit our time and resources to locking in on God, then He becomes apparent. The fruit of the spirit grows, and suddenly our eyes and ears are opened. When we seek, we will find (Matthew 7:7). God will reveal Himself when we prepare our hearts to receive Him.

So consider these questions for introspection:

1. Where are you seeing God at work in your life?
2. What steps are you taking to prepare your soul to receive God's Word?

3. Which soil type predominates in your
   heart today?

The seed of God's Word is constantly being spread. Are you seeing God in action? Are you hearing His message for you? Do you sense the moving of the Holy Spirit within you?

Until we prepare our heart to thrive on the nourishment of God's Word, we will have eyes but not see; we will have ears but not hear. May we set aside time to genuinely seek Him. Then, as written in 2 Peter 3:18, we will grow in grace and knowledge. Our efforts will not be in vain.

JESUS SAYS I AM HIS PEARL

Matthew 13:45–46

Have you ever wondered what Heaven is like? Typically, our thoughts gravitate to physical descriptions of the new Heaven, as pictured in Revelation 21: streets of gold, giant pearl gates, sparkling jewels and gems. But Jesus described the abstract aspects of Heaven in a series of parables in Matthew 13. Each parable begins with, "Heaven is like…" Then Jesus explained what Heaven is like. For example, Heaven is like separating wheat from weeds, or collecting good fish and culling out the bad. He explained that Heaven is expansive, like a giant tree growing from a tiny mustard seed and that Heaven is like a hidden treasure (Matthew 13:24–52).

Today, we focus on one of those parables of Jesus, describing a facet of Heaven. In Matthew 13:45–46, Jesus explained, "Again, the Kingdom of Heaven is like a merchant looking for fine pearls. When he found one of great value he went away and sold everything he had and bought it." In that parable, you and I are the pearls of great value.

God "went away" from Heaven—came to earth in the form of Jesus—and gave everything He had in order to acquire us as His own.

Heaven, therefore, is the gathering of souls—pearls of great value—who have been purchased at great cost by God. But most of us don't consider ourselves to be a pearl of great value. Perhaps it helps if we think about how pearls are made. Natural pearls are formed in an oyster shell and begin as a simple irritation. The oyster provides material from its own body to cover the irritant converting it, layer by layer, into a thing of beauty.

When we accept Jesus as Lord over our life, our sinful thoughts, words, and deeds—irritants to a Holy God—are covered with the lasting beauty of Jesus. As Christians, we strive to take on the character of Jesus, so that His luster is apparent in our words and actions—so that when people look at us, they see Jesus.

God looks beyond our current shortcomings. He sees our potential because He established the plans for our life. Psalm 139:16 reminds us that God saw us before our body was formed; He ordained our days before even one of them came to be. He sees beyond the present. He has specific plans for our life. And as we heed the leading of the Holy Spirit, we begin to grow into that God given potential.

There are times when I find it extremely difficult to see great value in some people. I see them simply as irritants. I don't see Jesus' covering on them. And I can't see what God might have planned for their life.

Perhaps that's why I'm not to judge the worth of people (Matthew 7:1). That is God's call, not mine. He can better understand the plans He has for each of us. He sees the value He has created in us. My job is to respect God's judgment and try to understand things from His perspective. The apostle Paul admonished new Christians, "from now on regard no one from a worldly point of view" (2 Corinthians 5:16).

In His parable, Jesus said that the pearl merchant "went away and sold everything he had in order to buy the valuable pearl." God paid dearly for us (John 3:16, 1 Corinthians 6:20). In fact, while we were still sinners—irritants—Jesus paid the ultimate price for us. He brought those who accept Jesus as Lord permanently into God's family (Romans 5:8, 1 Peter 1:18–19).

Realizing that God, at great expense, has purchased us and considers us to be pearls of great value, consider these questions for introspection:

1. When you encounter a person who irritates you, what helps you visualize that person as having great value to God?
2. God is like a pearl merchant who sold everything that was of value to him in order to buy a pearl of great value. What does that suggest to you about your worth to God?
3. God views you as a pearl of great value. What response does that motivate you to make?

Sometimes it's difficult for us to grasp the magnitude of the sacrifice that God has made for each of us. Having allowed Jesus to suffer for our sins so that you and I could spend eternity with God means that God places great value on each of us.

The depth of God's love naturally draws us to Jesus. And as we learn more about Jesus and as we assume greater degrees of His likeness and character, we receive the luster of a pearl of great value.

JESUS' HARVEST

Matthew 13:24–30

This week's scripture comes from Matthew 13:24–30. It is the first in a series of descriptions given by Jesus, explaining what Heaven is like. As was His custom, Jesus used a parable—an analogous story—to paint a picture in the minds of those who heard Jesus speak. A little later in Matthew's account we read the interpretation that Jesus gave to His disciples (Matthew 13:36–43).

Jesus began, "The Kingdom of Heaven is like a man who sowed good seed in his field." In the explanation given to His disciples, Jesus said that He was the one sowing good seed in His field. Jesus, as creator of this world (see John 1:1–3), owns the field and He plants His people here. The seed He broadcasts on earth are godly people, members of His Kingdom (Matthew 13:38).

But shortly after Jesus planted His people on this earth, an enemy—Satan—planted people who would pursue the devil's plan of disruption. Those who did the devil's work were the weeds in Jesus' parable (Matthew 13:38–39). Eradicating the weeds—the people of bad influence—while Christians were growing in the same field would potentially harm God's people. Therefore, both good and evil were allowed to grow side by side, until the time of harvest. Harvest would come, Jesus said, at the "end of the age," i.e., at the end of time when Heaven and earth are remade (Matthew 13:39, Revelation 21).

At the end of time, angels are sent to harvest what has grown on earth (Matthew 13:39–41, Revelation 14:14–20). They pull the weeds, gathering up all who follow the evil one, and throw them into the burning fires of hell. The followers of Jesus, however, will be gathered together into the Kingdom of righteousness (Matthew 13:43).

Heaven, therefore, separates good from evil. But here on earth, the good and the bad grow side by side. Both have been planted and both receive God's rain and sunshine (Matthew 5:45). You and I do not get to pass judgment, separating the good from the bad. That is reserved for God. Matthew 7:1 admonishes us, "Do not judge." And Matthew 5:39, 44 hold that we are to live in love, even in the midst of those who wrong us.

So in this passage we learn that Heaven is God's time and place for separating good and evil, but while we're on earth, the good grow in the midst of evil. Weeds will attempt to choke out or stunt the growth of God's crops. But as citizens of God's Kingdom, we are to grow in love, not allowing Satan's evil to provoke us into becoming vindictive or influenced by evil.

Accordingly, we sometimes find that we are planted among those who hate God's order and seek to divide and destroy one another. We are nevertheless called to express love—not by succumbing to evil's influence, but by promoting truth in love (Ephesians 4:15).

As we consider God's order and His plan for eternity, let's consider these questions for self-reflection:

1. The weeds of destructive behavior seem particularly prevalent in the world today. How are you growing in love, notwithstanding the divisive actions in our midst?
2. How does Christ's explanation of the big picture help you endure hardships caused by evil's growth?
3. God established a plan for everything from the beginning of time. You are part of that plan. What steps are you taking to become everything that God intended for you when He planted you here?

Often, we wonder why the influences of evil and its resultant infliction of pain and sickness are allowed here on earth. Jesus taught that evil would be destroyed ultimately but for now would not be weeded out because doing so could harm God's people.

Meanwhile, we are encouraged to grow in love, resisting the temptation to succumb to the harmful effects of evil. Knowing God's design and purpose for Heaven helps us resist the weeds that sometimes surround us. God has planned for us from the beginning of time. May we find strength and encouragement in His plan.

JESUS WARNS
AGAINST GREED
Luke 12:18–21

The author and preacher David Platt speaks of the conversation he has with believers as he travels across the United States. He asks the question, "Why do you suppose that God has allowed you to live in America—the most prosperous land in the history of the world?" The response that Platt typically receives is, "Gee, I guess that God has planted me in America because He loves me." Then Platt offers an alternative explanation. God has put us in this country so that resources are available to us for doing God's will. He explains, God has provided excess, not so we could *have* more, but so we could *give* more. Jesus put it this way, "From everyone who has been given much, much will be demanded" (Luke 12:48).

The text for consideration today is Luke 12:16–21, the parable of the rich fool. In this story Jesus describes a person who already had plenty and whose fields once again yielded a bountiful crop. The man thought to himself, *What shall I do? I have no place to store my crops.* Then he said, "I know what I'll do. I'll tear down my barns and build bigger ones, and there I will store my surplus grain."

Today as we hear Jesus' parable, we perhaps recognize the folly of hoarding more than we need. But do you know that here in America the storage-unit business has become a thirty-eight-billion-dollar industry? One out of every eleven Americans rents storage space to house their excess stuff. For many, the right to pursue happiness has been translated into an American dream of acquiring more things for ourselves.

The person in Jesus' parable expected to find security in his stockpile of grain that would supply his needs for many years. "I'll be able to take life easy: eat, drink, and be merry," he said. But then Jesus reached the point of His story, "God said to the man, 'you fool, this very night your life will be demanded from you, then who will get what you have prepared for yourself?'" (Luke 12:20).

In his self-centeredness, the man had expected to be set up forever, but instead he entered eternity empty-handed, leaving his stored-up assets behind. Elsewhere Jesus instructed, "Do not store up for yourselves treasures on earth, where moth and vermin destroy, and where thieves break in and steal. But store up for yourselves treasures in Heaven…for where your treasure is, there your heart will be also" (Matthew 6:19–21).

True security is found in storing up treasures in Heaven, rather than hoarding resources for ourselves here on earth. So how do we place our resources in Heaven?

Sending resources to Heaven means investing in God's Kingdom while we are living in the world. Everything we have comes from God. His is our provider (Luke 12:24, Philippians 4:19). By prioritizing our time, attention, and resources to focus first and foremost on God's priorities, we become invested in the eternal. Conversely, we can spend our God given time, attention, and resources on the temporary pleasures of this world, forgoing the opportunity to enter eternity invested in God's Kingdom.

Spending on God's priorities includes providing for the poor; it includes extending kindness to strangers and demonstrating compassion for the lonely, sick, and imprisoned. Jesus said an inheritance awaits them in Heaven (Matthew 25:34–36). In the final description of Heaven, Jesus explained that He provides rewards in eternity according to what we have done on earth to invest in God's priorities (Revelation 22:12). Therefore—back to the parable of Jesus—only a fool stores up things for himself without investing in God's eternal kingdom (Luke 12:21).

Hoarding comes naturally. We tend to be self-centered. We gather things up and hold onto them just in case we might need them. In its extreme, hoarding is recognized as a psychiatric disorder.

And holding on to money can become an obsession that blocks abundant living now and eternally. I had a college professor who liked to say that money is like manure. It does no good in a pile; it must be spread around to accomplish good.

Matthew 19:21 records a particularly blunt conversation that Jesus had with a person who was emotionally attached to his possessions but hoped to receive eternal life.

"Go sell your possessions and give to the poor and you will have treasure in Heaven," Jesus explained.

In another passage, Jesus instructed us to expend our resources on those who cannot reciprocate. "Although they cannot repay you, you will be repaid at the resurrection of the righteous" (Luke 14:14). But if our motive in giving is to receive accolades from others here on earth, then no investment is made in heaven because the praise of others will be our sole reward (Matthew 6:1–4).

Since we are citizens of Heaven (Philippians 3:20), our focus needs to be on the interests of God's Kingdom as opposed to earthly things. Advancing God's message by providing good works and being generous is listed in 1 Timothy 6:19 as a way to lay up treasures in God's Heavenly Kingdom.

So consider these questions for introspection:

1. List three ways that you could use your God-given resources to demonstrate Christ's compassion in this world.
2. What excess are you storing that could be better used by others?
3. The time we've been given on earth is a gift from God. How are we using that gift to promote His Kingdom?

Scripture does not require that we live an ascetic life of poverty. In fact, Jesus came to earth so that we might have abundant life (John 10:10). But as Christians we are called to be selfless—that was the example of Jesus who laid down His life for us. Second Corinthians 8:9 explains, "though He was rich, yet for your sake [Jesus] became poor, so that you through His poverty might become rich." Jesus gave up His Heavenly power and material comforts in order to come to earth to pay for our sins so that you and I might experience the riches of living in God's Kingdom for eternity.

Lord, help us to overcome the natural proclivity to horde your material blessings. Help us to be generous, investing in Your Heavenly Kingdom while we can.

JESUS TEACHES COMPASSION

Luke 16:19–31

Earthly blessings are made to be shared. Jesus taught us that how we share food and clothing with those who are in need and how we share our time with those who are sick or in prison will affect our destiny in the afterlife because how we handle earthly blessings is a reflection of our true belief in Jesus as Lord (Matthew 25:31–46). Today we look at Jesus' parable about the rich man and the beggar, recorded in Luke 16:19–31.

In the parable, Jesus spoke of a rich man who dressed in fine clothes and ate well. Just outside the gate to the rich man's house lay a beggar named Lazarus who was covered in sores. He was starving and in need of care. Lazarus would have relished eating even the crumbs left over from the rich man's meals. But the rich man ignored Lazarus every day.

In the story Lazarus and the rich man both died. Lazarus was taken to heaven and was received into the company of his ancestors. The rich man, however, was sent to Hades. From his place of torment, the rich man could see Lazarus being loved and cared for. The tables had been reversed, and now the rich man longed for even drippings of water that might come from Lazarus.

But the patriarch Abraham in Heaven explained to the rich man that a great permanent chasm had grown between the rich man and those in Heaven. The rich man's self-centered actions on earth had separated him from the eternal blessings of Heaven. He was distressed by his unalterable plight. But he had brothers who were still alive on earth. So the rich man asked Father Abraham to send Lazarus back to earth to warn his brothers about the pain that awaits those who selfishly hoard their blessings; then at least they could avoid hell.

But Abraham responded, "If your brothers are not heeding the warnings from Moses and the prophets, they likely would ignore a message even from someone who was risen from the dead" (Luke 16:31).

Did you notice in this parable that Jesus gave a name to the poor man, Lazarus, but the rich man was nameless? The rich man was anonymous. He was a nobody in Heaven. The book of life did not list the rich man's name.

Revelation 20:11–15 describes the final judgment of mankind. The dead are lined up before the great white throne of judgment and "were judged according to what they had done as recorded in the books" (Revelation 20:12). But wait! Redemption is a gift. We cannot earn our salvation. Romans 10:8 says the only requirement for entrance into heaven is that we "declare with our mouth that Jesus is Lord and believe in our heart that God raised Him from the dead."

Jesus' brother, James, explained that true belief in Jesus is life changing and is reflected in our actions. Even

Satan's demons believe that Jesus exists (James 2:18–19). But believing Jesus to be Lord over our life and claiming His sacrifice and resurrection as the atoning act for our soul will make us a changed person—one who has compassion for others, as Christ has had compassion for us. The true believer provides for those in need and expends time on behalf of the sick and imprisoned (Matthew 25:31–46).

Jesus' parable was bleak. He was confronting the listeners with the stark reality that we are blessed to be a blessing. And if we shirk our responsibility, that reflects our true heart. The apostle Paul explained to the early church in Corinth that "God is able to bless you abundantly, so that in all things at all times, having all that you need, you will abound in every good work." To that he added, "You will be enriched in every way so that you can be generous on every occasion" (2 Corinthians 9:8–11).

God provides for us, not so that we can lavish blessings on ourselves, but so that we can freely share with others. The compassion we demonstrate for others reveals our true belief in Jesus as our Lord and personal savior. The prophet Isaiah wrote that the Lord calls the redeemed by name (Isaiah 43:1). He knows His people and calls them by name (John 10:3). Their names are listed in the book of life (Revelation 20:15).

How does this parable about judgment and the need for compassion speak to you? Reflect on these questions if you will:

1. How have you experienced God's compassion?

2. How are you responding to the needs of others? Are you sharing your time, attention, and resources with those whom God has placed in your path?

3. Matthew 7:21–23 says that many will profess to be Christians but only those who "do the will of God" will be known by Jesus. When you are called into eternity and your actions examined, will your name be listed as one who exhibited the compassion of Christ? Is your name known in Heaven?

During His lifetime, Jesus taught that His disciples would be known by their Christlike loving actions (John 13:35). If Jesus is Lord over our life, then our everyday actions will reflect that. Too often our inclination is to ignore the needs of others. But Jesus set the example; you and I are called to live lives of compassion.

The time for compassion is now. Needs of others are presented to us every day. But the opportunity for service to others ends when we gasp our last breath on earth. May we spend our time on this planet wisely, glorifying God through acts of compassion.

JESUS BRINGS PEACE IN A TROUBLED WORLD

John 16:22–24

As the time for His crucifixion approached, Jesus fore-warned His followers that a time was coming when the disciples would grieve while the world rejoiced. But their time of grief, like birth pains, would usher in a new life—a life led by the Holy Spirit who would bring joy and power to the followers of Jesus (John 16:20–23).

Jesus explained to his disciples that they would be hated by the world because Jesus was hated by the world (John 15:18–21). They would be out of step—out of place—with the world's ways. But those who put their faith in Jesus would be empowered by the Holy Spirit, which would tes-tify about Jesus (John 15:26). Through faith in Jesus and the leading of the Holy Spirit, their time of suffering would evolve into a time of joy and power. Jesus promised that the Holy Spirit would guide the disciples through times of trouble (John 16:1–11).

Today, the crucifixion and resurrection of Jesus have already taken place. The Holy Spirit has arrived for believers. Just as Jesus promised, the Holy Spirit dwells within believers (1 Corinthians 3:16) and brings the peace of God that transcends all human understanding (Philippians 4:7). The Spirit now guides us through times of trouble, leading us through pain and into the joy of His presence.

Jesus gave the reason for this teaching, "I have told you these things so that in me you may have peace. In this world you will have trouble. But take heart! I have overcome the world!" (John 16:33).

What a timely reminder! In this world we will have trouble, but by following the Spirit's lead and focusing our attention on Jesus we can live in peace. Today trouble is exploding on every horizon. The pandemic, the reign of anarchists, the destruction of businesses and buildings and monuments, world unrest, climate change, and natural disasters—the list is endless. But in Jesus we find peace and a knowledge that He prevails in the end.

Jesus knew, of course, that a detailed plan has existed from the beginning of creation. He explicitly foretold the very kinds of troubles that now plague the world (Matthew 24). Yet He offered a solution. Be ready; be vigilant. Be led by the Holy Spirit (Matthew 25:36–51).

Jesus added that God would provide whatever we asked in Jesus' name (John 16:23). Praying in the name of Jesus means praying His will, not ours. It means viewing situations from Christ's point of view. It means taking on the appearance and actions of Christ. God answers our prayers, not because Jesus intervenes on our behalf, but because God appreciates the relationship we have with His Son, Jesus (John 16:26–27).

As I began preparing this meditation, Linda and I drove to Boston to pack out the apartment that our daughter-in-law had to leave when she returned to China due to the coronavirus pandemic. We gladly made the trip and closed out her apartment because of the relationship that she has with our beloved son. We love her because she loves our son. And therefore, we will undertake whatever she needs.

Jesus seemed to be making a similar point when He described God's answering our prayers that invoke the name and attitude of His Son, Jesus. Christians are referred to as the body of Christ (1 Corinthians 12:27) and the bride of Christ (Revelation 19:7–10). Our relationship with God's Son is what enables us to have direct access to God (John 16:26–27). God loves us and answers our prayers because of the relationship that we have with His beloved Son.

Therefore, in the midst of worldly challenges, we can find peace when we call out to God, in the name (and character) of Jesus. We know that our prayers are heard because we love God's Son, Jesus. Our relationship with Christ gives us the ear of God.

So consider these questions for introspection as we face the troubles of this world.

1. Philippians 4:6–9 instructs us to lift our concerns in prayer, with an attitude of thanksgiving, then the peace of God that defies human understanding will come upon us. Are you giving thanks in the midst of the troubles being dished out by the world?

2. Blessings in the midst of harshness are promised to those who faithfully follow God's instructions (Deuteronomy 11:13–14). What are you doing to learn and follow God's instructions?

3. God answers prayers for those who are committed to His Son, Jesus. How are you strengthening your relationship with Jesus?

In this world we will experience trouble. Jesus said so. And today we most certainly see trouble encircling the globe. But for those who have a meaningful relationship with Jesus, who listen for the still small voice—the voice of God's Holy Spirit, and who focus on God's instructions for life, they will find peace and joy. God's strength will come upon us, lifting as on wings of eagles (Isaiah 40:31), soaring above the whirlwind of earth's turmoil.

JESUS WAS BETRAYED

Matthew 26:15, 56, 69–75; 27:1–10

Have you ever been betrayed? I expect that we've all had that experience. We consider someone to be a trusted friend but then experience the painful disappointment of betrayal when they unexpectantly turn against us.

Jesus was betrayed by Judas Iscariot. Jesus had accepted Judas into the inner circle of disciples. He had entrusted Judas with authority to heal and to drive out evil spirits (Matthew 10:1). Judas, like all the disciples, was empowered by Christ to preach the Gospel message (Mark 3:14, Luke 9:1–2). Yet Judas turned against Jesus by providing the positive identification needed so that Jesus would not slip away from the angry mob as He had done on previous occasions (as in Luke 4:30, John 8:58–59, John 10:39).

But Jesus was not taken by surprise by Judas's betrayal. He saw this one coming. Jesus knew what was happening within each person (John 2:25). In fact, in the case of Judas, Jesus knew from the beginning that Judas would betray Him (John 6:64). Jesus watched as Satan's influence grew within Judas. He was aware of Judas stealing from the disciples' moneybag, and He witnessed Judas criticize acts of grace, disguising the criticism by falsely asserting that he had a desire to serve the poor (John 12:6).

Jesus, nevertheless, gave Judas every opportunity to turn from his worldly ways and grow as a disciple. He shared with Judas the details of the ministry. He entrusted Judas with responsibility in the ministry. He even washed Judas's feet at the Last Supper (John 13:4–5). But Judas had given Satan a foothold in his soul, and the evil influence grew unchecked, until Judas openly turned against Jesus. At the Last Supper Jesus announced that Judas's betrayal was about to happen (John 13:26–27).

If it had been only Judas who betrayed Christ, that would have been bad enough, but Peter publicly disavowed even knowing Jesus (Matthew 26:69–75). And the disciples scattered once Jesus had been taken (Matthew 26:56, Mark 14:50). Most of His closest colleagues betrayed Him.

Jesus experienced betrayal. He knew the pain of rejection. Nevertheless, He went to the cross willingly, to cover the sins of the world, even for those who had turned on Him. Just as Jesus became a servant to Judas and the rest of the disciples, washing their feet and dying for their sins, He has suffered and died on our behalf.

This scenario of betraying Jesus reoccurs in life every day. Jesus knows our heart. He sees when we allow Satan to have a foothold within us, harboring ill will toward another, passing judgment, twisting scripture, avoiding Christ for the sake of political correctness. Jesus sees the folly of our ways and the betrayal in our hearts, yet He waits patiently to receive us if only we will turn to Him.

Satan prowls like a hungry lion, looking for souls to devour (1 Peter 5:8). Resist him (1 Peter 5:9). Do not give Satan a foothold in your life (Ephesians 4:27). Because when we give in, just a little bit to sin's lure, next time it's more difficult to resist. Eventually, yielding to Satan's ways becomes natural, a way of life, and our hearts become hardened to Jesus' call.

It's never too late to rebuff Satan and to turn over every aspect of our life to Jesus. But the longer we put it off, the more difficult it becomes. If we don't nip it in the bud, Satan's grip can come into full bloom of open defiance against godly living.

We tend to rationalize our way into trouble: what difference will it make if my language is a little salty? Who cares if I stretch the truth to make my point? No one will notice if I take this thing that does not belong to me. I'll just disavow this part of scripture; after all, I don't want to hurt anyone's feelings with the harsh truth (that coincidently may send them to hell for eternity).

In life we have choices. We can choose to follow the world's dictates, or we can follow scripture. In 1 John 2:15–17 we read, "Do not follow the world or anything in the world…for anyone who [follows] the world, the love of the Father is not in them." The repeating theme of the book of Judges is that in the absence of spiritual direction "everyone did as they saw fit," which resulted in disaster and chaos (Judges 17:6). Scripture is given to us for instruction (2 Timothy 3:16).

While being betrayed, Jesus went to the cross. He suffered for the sake of His betrayers—betrayers that sometimes include you and me. So consider these questions, if you will, for introspection:

1. Ephesians 4:27 instructs us to refuse to give Satan a foothold in our life. What are some examples of refusing to give Satan a foothold in your life?

2. It's never too late to turn to Jesus, and that begins by acknowledging our betrayals to Him and promising to change. Do your prayers include confession and repentance?

3. In the Old Testament story of Joseph who wore a coat of many colors, Joseph experienced the pain of rejection and betrayal at the hands of his brothers. Years later he was able to recognize that God had not abandoned him but had been at work even during the betrayal by his brothers (Genesis 50:20). When have you experienced betrayal and how was God at work then?

Jesus knows our heart (John 2:25). Yet we are instructed to confess our wrongdoings (Proverbs 28:13, James 5:16, 1 John 1:9). Through confession and repentance, our relationship with Christ is restored (Acts 3:19).

When Jesus defeated sin's penalty of death, He came back to the disciples. Although He had experienced the disappointment of betrayal, He visited with Peter so that Peter could return to the work of God's Kingdom (John 21:15–17). He appeared to doubting Thomas so that Thomas would not be lost (John 20:24–29). And He returns—in the Holy Spirit—to you and to me.

Scripture promises that God never leaves us nor turns against us (Deuteronomy 31:6, Hebrews 13: 5). Despite our acts of betrayal that no doubt disappoint our Savior, He is always there for us, waiting patiently for our acknowledgment that we've let Him down but that we've resolved to more closely track His teaching and His example. God will lead us in paths of restoration if we are open to it.

JESUS TEACHES US TO SEEK GOD

Matthew 7:7–12

In the summer of 2018, thirteen members of a youth soccer club in Thailand became lost in a cave that flooded, trapping the youth and their coach some two and one-half miles in from the entrance. While the boys were desperately seeking a way out, scores of searchers were frantically seeking a way in to rescue the team. Many hours of intense seeking were finally rewarded with a successful rescue. With any lesser effort, the boys would have been lost as the waters closed in and the oxygen supply dwindled.

In the Sermon on the Mount, Jesus provided instruction about "seeking." "Ask and it will be given to you, seek and you will find, knock and the door will be opened for you" (Matthew 7:7). To that He added, "Everyone who asks receives; the one who seeks finds; and to the one who knocks the door will be opened" (Matthew 7:8).

Jesus was encouraging His listeners to pursue God. He was assuring them that their diligent efforts in seeking God would not be in vain.

Often, we hear people lament that they don't find God in their life. They don't see God at work in their midst and certainly can't find Him in the tumult and divisions of today's culture. Why is that? Why is God not found? Why is He elusive for so many?

The Old Testament character, Job, endured many tragedies in his life. He complained, "If I go to the east [God] is not there, if I go to the west, I do not find Him. When He is at work in the north, I do not see Him; when He turns to the south, I catch no glimpse of Him" (Job 23:8–9). What makes Job remarkable is that despite his inability to see God in his presence, Job remained confident that God was aware of what was going on (Job 23:10).

Job's difficulty in seeing God's presence describes the perception of many people today. Trouble seems pervasive. And God is not easily found in any of it. Yet Jesus promised that those who seek God will find Him. Why does God seem elusive? And how can we seek Him more effectively?

There are probably many explanations for our losing sight of God in our everyday life. Often, we're just too busy to seek Him. Or the time we spend looking for God is half-hearted. We may attend an occasional Bible study and may listen to a sermon or two covering parts of scripture, but life gets in the way. Perhaps that's why, for many, earnest seeking of God does not take place until life has spiraled out of control. When we're down and out, feeling like everything is lost, that's often the time that searching for God becomes a higher priority.

I'd like to offer four suggestions for following Christ's directive to seek God.

Suggestion number one is that we seek God as if our life depended on it. Effectively seeking God requires us to be unabashed and vigorous in our search. King David instructed his son Solomon to seek God with wholehearted devotion; the king promised that if Solomon did so, he would find God at work in his life. (1 Chronicles 28:9). And Solomon, in his wisdom, exhorted the people to seek God with the passion of a lover (Proverbs 8:17).

Jesus instructed us to "seek first the Kingdom of God," i.e., make that our number one priority (Matthew 6:33). And the advice given through Moses was "You will find God if you seek Him with all your heart and with all your soul" (Deuteronomy 4:29). Like the efforts employed in seeking a rescue for the Thai soccer club, our efforts in seeking God need to be exercised with an enthusiasm that suggests that finding Him is essential to sustaining our life—because it is. (John 14:1-4). Our eternal life depends on finding God.

Suggestion number two is that we never give up; never stop seeking God. Winston Churchill's advice given during World War Two, in a speech at the Harrow School, was "never give in." Likewise, James instructed that persistence wins the day. He wrote, "The one who perseveres under trial…will receive the crown of life" (James 1:12). And in the Olivet Discourse, Jesus spoke of exercising persistence during these end times. He taught, "the one who stands firm to the end will be saved" (Matthew 24:13).

My third suggestion is to fellowship with believers. Your mother was correct when she told you to be careful about whom you associate with because you tend to take on the characteristics of those with whom you spend time. The writer of Hebrews subscribed to the practice of spending time with other believers. Do not neglect meeting together and encouraging one another was his advice (Hebrews 10:25).

And fourth, learn to trust your Bible. Your Bible is the inspired instruction from God (2 Timothy 3:16). The psalmist wrote, "All your words are true; all your righteous laws are eternal" (Psalm 119:160). But Satan's ancient ploy is often used today: "did God really say that?" (Genesis 3:1). Satan, the great deceiver, eagerly twists scripture in an effort to lead people away from God. The apostle Paul cautioned, "Just as Eve was deceived by the serpent's cunning, your minds may be led astray" (2 Corinthians 11:3).

Every pilot learns to trust the instruments in her aircraft. Her life depends on it. There are times when an airplane flies into clouds, and the pilot loses her frame of reference and then can easily become disoriented. That's when the pilot's training kicks in: trust your instruments. In life-troubling circumstances our view can become clouded. Satan seizes those opportunities to create doubt: "Did God really say that?" That's when our Bible training needs to kick in. God's Word is inspired, true, and reliable.

Seeking God requires diligent effort and persistence. Fellowship with other believers and God's inspired manual for life are aids in our efforts to seek God. So consider, if you will, these questions for introspection:

1. How are you currently seeking God?
2. Do you regularly meet with a Christian mentor, or do you participate in an accountability group?

3. What steps are you taking to build up
   your knowledge of scriptures?

The Bible assures us that God is always present. He's with us even in the toughest of times. (See, e.g., the promises of Isaiah 41:10, Deuteronomy 31:6, Hebrews 13:5.) But often His presence is obscured until we seek Him with great fervor and persistence, much like the efforts that were put forth to save the Thai soccer club. Seeking God requires us to pursue Him as if our life depended on finding Him because our eternal life does depend on finding Him.

The tools for our seeking God are as near as our Bible and our Christian friends. Employ both regularly and earnestly. Seeking God will not take place without our conscious decisions to study our Bible and discuss our Christian walk with fellow believers. The circumstances of this world tend to pull us away from seeking God; Satan is doing everything he can to divert our attention and consume our time with worry and anxiety.

Jesus, of course, was right. If we will truly seek God, we will find Him in our midst.

JESUS' TEACHING ON WORRY AND ANXIETY

Matthew 6:25–34

Worry cannot change the past nor can it alter the future, but it can needlessly destroy the present. Worry just may be one of Satan's favorite tools. Worry often wastes its energy on things that may never happen, things that we cannot control, and things that don't matter in the long run—that is in the eternal life of our soul.

But worry is a fact of life. Humans tend to worry. Anxiety is easily provoked, leading to ulcers, heart issues, sleeplessness, unhealthy eating habits, and other deleterious conditions. Anxiety and its harmful effects are ravaging people today. Like a merry-go-round gone mad, the same worries keep revolving in our mind, playing over and over. That's when we need to focus our attention on the good and noble things in life (Philippians 4:8).

A friend used to say, "don't rehearse it, reverse it." That is, don't reinforce the worries by repeating them in your mind. Instead, reverse things by concentrating on God's goodness. Because life will unfold exactly as it's going to despite our excess stomach acid and sleepless nights.

Early in His ministry, Jesus instructed, "Do not worry about your life, what you will eat or drink, or about your body, what you will wear" (Matthew 6:25). His logic, of course, was unassailable. God who created us can be trusted with the details of our lives, and worrying only gets in the way of His plans for us. Moreover, faith in God means resting in His providence.

Those who know me best realize that Jesus' instruction about worry is my all-time favorite passage of scripture. That's because in the spring of 1987 I was busy with work. Often, I was too busy for family; I was too busy for Bible study; and I was too busy for meaningful relationships. That is until suddenly the firm where I worked went out of business.

At that time when I was facing mounting debt, no income, and no work, several people directed me to Matthew 6:25–34. In that passage Jesus explained that worry was a waste of time; it was counterproductive. "Seek first God's Kingdom," He said, then everything will fall into place (Matthew 6:33). I gave it a try. Sure enough, by working on a relationship with Jesus, lifting my concerns to Him, I eventually was able to view life's circumstances more from His perspective. His order came into my world.

Years later, I came to appreciate a friend's approach to troubles that would crop up. Rather than getting bothered with worry, she'd exclaim, "I can't wait to see what God does with this!"

Christians are not spared the troubles of this world, but by following Christ's directions, they can be relieved of the destructive forces of anxiety and worry. So let's dig a little deeper into the antidote that Jesus prescribed for worry.

"Seek first the Kingdom of God" (Matthew 6:33). Jesus understood that we have basic human needs of food, shelter, and clothing but when we begin to obsess on those needs, He instructed us to seek Him and His truth. In place of worries about worldly things, He instructed us to delve into a more meaningful relationship with God. Focus on His creation and provision. From that relationship we can gain heavenly perspective, recognizing that God provides for plants and animals in the natural order of things and that He values us even more. Therefore, we can count on God making provisions for each of us; after all, we are beings created in God's own image and designed for fellowship with His Son, Jesus (Genesis 1:27; 1 Corinthians 1:9).

When Jesus instructed that we seek first the Kingdom of God, He was telling us to allow God to be king over our life. In God's Kingdom, His rules for living prevail. God's people—citizens of His Kingdom—are subject to His standards for morality and godly living. Becoming a citizen of God's Kingdom requires us to learn God's rules for life. In the context of His teaching, Jesus was telling us to subject ourselves to God's rule, rather than the rule of earthly mammon (Matthew 6:24).

Adherence to God's rules for living—instead of buckling to the worldly standards that are measured by money—naturally leads to our earthly needs being covered because

God, as creator of everything, has provided for all worldly needs (Philippians 4:19).

When one renounces his citizenship in one kingdom in order to declare loyalty to another, he first studies the standards of the kingdom as to which he is about to declare his loyalty. When a foreigner becomes a US citizen, he must first learn the standards that apply in this country. Citizenship in God's Kingdom requires us to study God's Word—the Bible—to understand God's ways.

Jesus was directing us, who are natural-born citizens of this sin-soaked world, to abdicate our loyalty to this world that is driven by money and greed, and instead subject ourselves to the divine standards of the one who created everything and who has supplied all that is needed for life. By changing our loyalty, we modify our focus, changing from earthly to Heavenly Kingdom standards.

So consider if you will these questions for introspection:

1. How are you seeking God first in your everyday living?
2. What citizenship training are you engaged in to help you acclimate to being a citizen of God's Kingdom?
3. When worry begins to crowd into your mind, what steps do you take to prevent it from overwhelming your mind and destroying the joys of today?

That old saying is true: "Yesterday is history, tomorrow a mystery. Today is a gift, that's why it's called the present." We waste our efforts when we worry about what has already happened, and we likewise waste our efforts when we worry about things that may never occur. Focusing on the gift of today is best done when we recognize God at work in the circumstances of the moment.

He is always present (Isaiah 43:2, Matthew 28:20), and He cares deeply about you (1 Peter 5:7). So push away Satan's trap of worry and instead seek a deeper relationship with the One who created you and who has provided for your needs.

JESUS TEACHES THE COST OF DISCIPLESHIP

Matthew 8:18–22

Becoming a disciple of Jesus is an ongoing process by which we grow in selflessness. Jesus was the ultimate example of selflessness. He had no earthly home for himself; He had no wardrobe other than the clothes He wore. His entire mission was focused on others, even to the point of giving His life for the sake of others.

Being a disciple means learning from and following the example of another—a teacher. It means serving an apprenticeship to emulate the qualities and characteristics of a master. A disciple of Jesus, therefore, is one who studies the principles that Jesus taught and follows His example in everyday living.

In Matthew 8:18–22, Jesus described the total commitment expected of those who claim to be His disciple. A crowd had gathered, but Jesus gave the order to "move on." He shunned the opportunity to bask in rock-star-type fame available from the crowd that had gathered. It was then that a teacher of the law approached Jesus and vowed to follow Jesus wherever He went (Matthew 8:19).

The eminent preacher, Charles Spurgeon, explained that this teacher of the law—a scribe—had already begun making a name for himself as evidenced by the fact that he bore the title "scribe." The scribe's knowledge of scripture would have far exceeded that of the uneducated disciples who accompanied Jesus. With his education, the scribe likely thought that he could rise to a position of importance in Jesus' ministry. And being associated with Jesus would enhance the scribe's reputation and status.

Jesus replied, "Foxes have dens and birds have nests, but the Son of Man has no place to lay His head" (Matthew 8:20). In effect, Jesus was telling the scribe, don't become a follower of me in order to increase your own fame and fortune. This ministry is about sacrificing self; it's the opposite of building ego.

Then another person approached Jesus and said that he would follow Jesus just as soon as he completed his responsibilities of burying his father. But the text does not say that the man's father had died or that his death was imminent. Nothing indicates that the man was in mourning or making funeral arrangements. Therefore, some commentators conclude that the man was saying that when he had completed his worldly responsibilities—in today's culture, reached retirement—then he would follow Jesus.

Jesus answered this man, "Follow me and let the dead bury their own dead" (Matthew 8:22). This sounds heartless, but Jesus was saying do not put off following Him, waiting until a more convenient time. Responsibilities of life are always present, crowding out time for spiritual growth.

In Luke 14:25–35, Jesus discussed the need to consider the cost of discipleship. Salvation is free, but discipleship costs everything. By accepting the free gift of salvation, we commit everything to Jesus. We make Him Lord over our life.

Claiming Jesus as Lord over our life is a decision that is not to be taken lightly. Sometimes claiming Jesus as Lord is an emotional response to temporary circumstances. But Jesus cautioned that being His disciple is an exercise of extreme selflessness. Being a disciple means committing everything we have and everything we've become to Him. It means placing our relationship with Christ above our family (Luke 14:26). It means daily dying to self, described by Jesus as "carrying our cross" (Luke 14:27). Being a disciple means making Jesus first and foremost in every aspect of our life (Matthew 8:22).

Some falsely believe that they can be a "light-duty Christian," one who accepts the free gift of salvation, but makes room for Christ only when it's convenient or easy. That is not discipleship. And if we're not willing to be a disciple of Jesus, then we've not really made Him Lord over our life. Yet that is the cost of accepting the free gift of salvation.

Jesus spoke of those who were adherents of Christ in name only. He said, "Not everyone who says to me 'Lord, Lord' will enter the Kingdom of Heaven, but only those who do the will of my Father" (Matthew 7:21). He told of the deep regrets of those who supposed that they were safe by identifying as Christians without committing themselves fully to His cause (Matthew 25:31–46). And Titus had harsh words for those who "claim to know God but by their actions deny him" (Titus 1:16).

Sober consideration is required for the decision to make Jesus Lord. If we are not willing to commit everything—our time, our resources, our talents—then are we truly disciples of Jesus? And if we are not disciples, then are we Christians in name only?

As we reflect on the cost of discipleship, consider these questions for introspection:

1. Jesus was a master of selflessness, freely giving His time, talent, and life for the benefit of others. Where is God calling you to grow in selflessness?
2. What prevents you from spending time studying and following Jesus?
3. Is Jesus truly Lord over all aspects of your life? In what areas do you tend to exclude Jesus?

If He is Lord, then everything about us is dedicated to His ministry. Time, talent, material comforts, and relationships all belong to Christ. Becoming His disciple is costly. Jesus encouraged His followers to give mature consideration to the cost of becoming a disciple.

Salvation is free. We cannot earn it. We do not deserve it. But once we accept Jesus' sacrifice on our behalf and become His disciple, His dedicated follower, then our life changes. We grow in selflessness, ever striving to be more Christlike in every aspect of our life. As His disciple, we declare, "Jesus is Lord."

JESUS TEACHES PRAYER

Matthew 6:5–15

Prayer is an essential building block in forming a relationship with God. Early in His ministry, Jesus taught about prayer. In fact, prayer was included in the basic instructions Jesus gave in the Sermon on the Mount (Matthew 6:5–15).

His teaching on prayer began with a directive that prayer is not to be done for the purpose of bringing public acclaim to the one offering prayer. Hypocrites do that, Jesus said (Matthew 6:5). Rather, prayer is intended to be an intimate conversation with God. Prayers can be lifted to God in a group setting, but the purpose is to bring glory to God, not to the one leading prayer.

And there is no need to ramble on in endless prayer. God already knows our needs, and He knows our heart (Matthew 6:8, Acts 15:8). Prayer, therefore, can be concise, crystallizing our concerns, which in turn allows us to focus on God's Holy Spirit leading in those areas. Listening, therefore, is part of prayer.

Then Jesus advised that we "begin like this: 'Our Father in Heaven...'" Let's stop right there! This is significant. Jesus was directing people to pray directly to God, referring to Him as "our Father." Jesus was God's Son (John 1:14), and scripture says that we too are sons and daughters of God (Matthew 12:50). That means that we are siblings of Christ (Romans 8:14-17), and God is our Father.

Before Jesus, mankind's relationship with God—our Father—had been blocked by sin. Access to God, therefore, required repeated intervention by earthly priests in the form of sin offerings (Leviticus 4:1–35). But Jesus was the permanent cover for our sins (John 1:29). At His death, the curtain in the temple that had separated the people from God was ripped open from the top to the bottom (Matthew 27: 51). When Heaven tore open the curtain that separated us from God, we then were given direct access to God. Because of Jesus' cover for our sins, we have permanent direct access to God and therefore pray directly to God, our Father in Heaven.

Jesus next instructed that we recognize God as being holy, "hallowed be thy name" (Matthew 6:9). *Hallow* is the old English word for holy. Being holy means being set apart as sacred and, in the case of God, being worthy of praise and exultation (Psalm 99:9).

Jesus then instructed that we ask that God's will be done on earth as it is done in His Heavenly Kingdom. If God were universally recognized as king here on earth, then all His subjects would adhere to His command to "love one another" (John 15:9–12). Ultimately, Heaven and earth will be consolidated and God's directive to love one another will be accepted and followed as the law of the land (Revelation 21:1–8).

Then Jesus said, pray for your needs for that day. When God provided manna from Heaven as sustenance for the wandering Hebrew nation, He was teaching them to focus on the current day. The manna was good only for that day (Exodus 16:20). We too are to focus on the present. It is a gift from God. That being said, we need to seek Him daily, not just once in a while. And we need to spend time listening for His direction. Relationships, after all, are not formed through occasional or one-way conversations.

Jesus continued, "ask that God forgive you for your sins, just like you forgive others who have sinned against you" (Matthew 6:12). Jesus added this explanation, "If you forgive other people when they sin against you, your heavenly father will also forgive you. But if you do not forgive others of their sins, your Father will not forgive you of yours" (Matthew 6:14–15). Prayer is not idle chatter; it has teeth. Jesus was making the point that we cannot get away with ignoring God's command to forgive.

Lastly, Jesus said ask that God provide an escape route that allows you to avoid Satan's traps. Life on this planet is fraught with temptation. Our human condition is to be self-centered. When we are caught up in pride, greed, and covetousness—the sins that are born out of selfishness—we are susceptible of being caught up in sin. God promises that He will provide a way of escape (1 Corinthians 10:13), but we need to be watching for it and need to be willing to take that escape route without hesitation or delay.

If we hope to have a relationship with God, then we must be willing to communicate with Him. No relationship is built without communication. And prayer is the means that has been provided for us to communicate with our Holy creator. Jesus set the example. He was in such constant prayer contact with God that he took on God's words and actions as His own (John 14:10–11).

So how about you? How is your prayer life? Let's reflect for a moment on these questions for introspection:

1. God is Holy. He is the almighty creator of the universe and at the same time is our Father. How would you describe the deference you give to God in your prayer conversations with Him?

2. What is God's will for you right now? Are you following His will or are you just mouthing empty words, "thy will be done"?

3. The apostle Paul frequently wrote "Grace be with you." (See, e.g., 1 Timothy 6:21; 2 Thessalonians 3:18.) Grace is undeserved blessing. Grace is forgiving, "cutting some slack" for offenders. Do you currently have an opportunity to offer grace—forgiveness—to someone who has offended you?

Prayer is a core component to building a relationship with God. Too often we delay prayer, deferring conversations with God until a time that is more convenient for us. As a result, prayer is sometimes postponed until we have become desperate.

Don't put off developing an intimate relationship with your Heavenly Father. He's always there, present in our midst. In the hustle of everyday living, He's waiting for our conversation with Him. He's ready to reveal perspective that will help us in those stressful times. He's standing by with daily provision, forgiveness, and direction. Reach out to Him in prayer.

JESUS TEACHES US TO WITNESS

John 4:1–26

In the Great Commission, Jesus instructed His followers to go and make disciples of all nations (Matthew 28:19). In that process, as members of the body of Christ, we are called to speak "truth in love" (Ephesians 4:15). Advancing the Gospel message can be bungled if we come across as being judgmental or display a "holier than thou" attitude. Jesus gave us an example of how to make disciples of other nations when He encountered the woman at the well as recorded in John 4:1–42.

On that occasion, Jesus was returning to Galilee (John 4:3). He decided to cut through Samaria—the territory occupied by the descendants of foreigners who had moved into the area and intermarried with the remaining Jews after the Assyrian army had conquered the northern kingdom of Israel (2 Kings 17:24). The Samaritans practiced a hybrid form of worship that recognized many gods and a hodgepodge of religious practices.

At midday, Jesus stopped by a well that had been dug centuries earlier by Jacob (Genesis 33:18–19). At that hottest point of the day no one was at the well—that is no one except a Samaritan woman who apparently was a social outcast in her Samaritan community. She had come to the well at the hottest point of the day, and that allowed her access the well without being subjected to the judgmental stares and comments of the other women who would be there at the cooler times of the day drawing water for their households.

Although it was against social norms for a rabbi to speak in public to a woman, and even more unacceptable for a Jew to speak to a Samaritan, Jesus approached the woman and asked, "Will you give me a drink?" The woman replied, "You are a Jew and I am a Samaritan woman. How can you ask me for a drink?" (John 4:9).

That's all it took to get the conversation started—a conversation between Jesus and a member of another nation. Jesus was not reticent about sharing the Gospel message. He replied, "If you knew the gift of God and who it is that asks you for a drink—that is if you knew Jesus—you would have 'living water'" (John 4:10). *Living water* was a term that had been used by the prophet Jeremiah to describe the hope available to those who lived by God's standards rather than by the polluted standards of the world (Jeremiah 2:13, 17:13).

The woman's curiosity had been piqued. Where can one get this living water? Are you able to provide even greater refreshment than Jacob who gave us this well? Jesus then led her deeper into the discussion by explaining that His living water led to eternal life (John 4:14).

When the Samaritan woman asked Jesus to supply her with living water, Jesus directed her to bring her husband to the meeting. The woman confessed that she had no husband. That was when Jesus confronted her with the fact that she was living with a man who was not her husband and that she had moved through five prior similar relationships.

To use current-day vernacular, the Samaritan woman had been looking for love in all the wrong places. She was searching for meaning in her life. She likely craved being valued as a person of worth. Her spirit was parched. She was feeling the despair that we sometimes experience when our life seems dehydrated and lifeless, routine but going nowhere.

Jesus had gently, but directly, addressed the "elephant in the room." He had drawn out an acknowledgment of the woman's sinful human condition. Uncomfortable with the attention on her lifestyle, the woman attempted to shift focus back to Jesus. "I see that you are a prophet," she said, "what do you think about the difference in worship practices between the Jews and the Samaritans?" (John 4:20).

Jesus then explained that the Samaritans were worshipping what they did not know, i.e., they were combining some of Moses's laws with the pagan practices of the local culture. But salvation and the Messiah would come from the Jews as promised by the Old Testament prophets of the one true God (John 4:21–22).

Then Jesus added, "God is spirit" and worship must be focused on the spirit and truth of God, not on the trappings of the culture or religious practices of the day (John 4:24). Then Jesus revealed to the woman that He was the promised Messiah (John 4:26). The woman went into town and shared what she had heard, and as a result many of the Samaritans believed in Jesus as the Messiah (John 4:39).

There are several takeaways for us in the story of the woman at the well:

1. Sharing the Gospel message begins with conversation. Jesus began the conversation with the Samaritan woman by asking for a favor. By asking for a favor, Jesus was disarming. He was the person in need and that allowed the woman to be less intimidated by the encounter and to be more open to the conversation.

2. As soon as they were engaged in conversation, Jesus brought up the good news of hope for a better life through the Messiah Jesus. As the Apostle Paul wrote, He was not ashamed of the Gospel (Romans 1:16). Jesus instructed His followers to not be ashamed of the Gospel, but to freely share it. (Mark 8:38, Luke 9:26).

3. Jesus spoke the truth in love. The woman brought up the fact that she was living in sin. Jesus did not condemn her, but neither did he countenance or approve

her sinful ways. Today's climate of political correctness suggests that we need to affirm lifestyles that violate the standards of scripture. That would be speaking lies rather than truth and lies come from Satan and his minion the anti-Christ, not from God. But neither do we get to pronounce judgment. Our calling is to speak truth in love (Ephesians 4:15).

4. Jesus spoke to the woman's spiritual thirst. Today's greatest epidemic is not coronavirus; it is spiritual emptiness. People are sensing an internal void that needs to be filled. Some turn to service projects, some turn to self-help books, and some turn to horoscopes and spiritual soothsayers. But only Jesus can fill that emptiness that plagues the world.

So as we strive to answer the call of the Great Commission to go make disciples of all nations, how are you doing? Reflect with me if you will on these questions for introspection:

1. Where would you be able to encounter someone from a different background with whom to share the Gospel message?
2. How would you begin a conversation that could lead to telling someone about Jesus?

3. What message would you share about Jesus?

The directive from Jesus is clear: we are to go make disciples of all nations (Matthew 28:19). But how many of us actually follow through on this one task that Jesus assigned to us?

When we become Christians, we are commissioned to be His messengers. We are to tell others about Jesus. That is an essential characteristic of being a Christian. So let's go tell others about Jesus.

JESUS TEACHES ABOUT SERVICE

Matthew 25:31–46

O ne of the most moving experiences of my life took place on a mountainside house lot in Appalachia. I was one of the adult chaperones for a team of teenagers who'd been dispatched to build a room addition on a mobile home that was occupied by a family in need. After several days of hard work, the room addition was taking shape. The family was so grateful that they insisted on providing lunch for us one day.

This family could barely afford to feed themselves, not to mention feeding a group of hungry teenagers. But that did not stop this family. Their feeding us was a natural outpouring of their gratitude. The family appeared not to think twice about it. And so we feasted on a delicious meal of wilted greens and chicken gizzards cooked in bacon fat.

In the twenty-fifth chapter of the book of Matthew, Jesus described the division that will take place at the time of judgment. True believers will be separated from fake ones. Of course, God knows everyone's heart (Acts 15:8), but Jesus explained that the difference could be seen in acts of service. Those who are welcomed into Heaven will be those who fed the hungry, clothed the naked, and visited inmates in prison (Matthew 25:34–37). Those who ignored the needs of others will be rejected.

But what is even more telling is that those who served others were not even aware of it. Service came naturally for those who gratefully received salvation and became disciples of Jesus. As they were entering the gates of Heaven, they were saying, "Lord, when did we see you hungry and feed you, or thirsty and give you something to drink?" And the King will reply, "Whatever you did for the least of these brothers and sisters, you did for me" (Matthew 25:37–40).

Entrance into heaven cannot be earned. We are saved by grace—undeserved blessing, and not by works (Ephesians 2:8–9). Yet Jesus pointed out that service is a distinguishing factor of those who enter Heaven.

Just as an apple tree can be identified by its fruit, so a believer can be identified by his or her acts of love (John 13:35). The fruit grows naturally, without thought. Christians, by their nature, are selfless, always looking for the opportunity to serve others.

So how do we reach that point of naturally pouring out grace to others? How do we become selfless like Jesus? What brings about the change in our heart and mind to put others' interests ahead of our own?

It's not by accident that we become new creations (2 Corinthians 5:17). It starts with a conscious decision. And being transformed into the likeness of Christ is a process.

If we study the descriptions of Jesus as reported in scripture, and if we strive to be more like Him, following His examples of selfless action, then when we encounter human need we sense His call to serve. When opportunities for service to others arise it's as if we hear Jesus saying, "Do you love me? Then feed my sheep."

At the end of His earthly ministry, the "bottom line" message that Jesus had for His lead disciple Peter was "If you love me, then serve those in need." Repeatedly, Jesus asked Peter, "Do you love me?" When Peter assured Jesus that he loved Him, Jesus responded, "Then feed my sheep," i.e., care for the lost, the least, the wandering souls in need of Jesus (John 21:15–17). Feeding those for whom Christ died consists of both physical feeding and spiritual feeding; man does not live on bread alone, but on every word that comes from God (Matthew 4:4). You and I are called into service to answer the physical and spiritual needs of a hungry world.

Human need is everywhere. And eventually, if we strive to be like Christ, we find ourselves naturally considering the welfare of others instead of being totally wrapped up in ourselves (Philippians 2:3–4). Reaching that point requires us to give up the priorities of this world in order to pursue God's plan for our life (Romans 12:2).

So consider these questions for introspection if you will:

1. What human need is speaking to you right now? This may be your call to action.
2. Each person who accepts Jesus as savior and Lord is the recipient of the gift of

eternal life (Romans 10:9). How are you expressing gratitude for the Heavenly gift that came from Jesus' sacrifice on the cross?

3. Disciples of Jesus are servants in training. What opportunities for service are available to you today?

When we truly love Jesus and accept Him as our Lord, then our natural response to the human condition that surrounds us is to selflessly serve those in need. It's not a matter of earning our way into Heaven, it's a matter of doing what comes naturally because Jesus has a heart for those in need, and you and I have been deputized into His service. We become the hands and feet of Jesus. As we serve the needs of others, we are acting for Jesus (Matthew 25:40, "whatever you did for one of the least of these your brethren...you did for me").

When Jesus calls us into service, it's not something to be ignored. Service opportunities do not always present themselves at convenient times. They often require personal sacrifice. But then Jesus set the example. His earthly service to you and me was neither convenient nor easy. Therefore, if we are following His example, we naturally serve others. The directive that sometimes has been attributed to John Wesley applies to each of us. We are to:

Do all the good you can,
By all the means you can,
In all the ways you can,

In all the places you can,
At all the times you can,
To all the people you can,
As long as ever you can.

JESUS LOVES ME

John 3:16

The best-known Bible verse is probably John 3:16: "For God so loved the world that He gave His one and only Son, that whosoever believes in Him shall not perish but have everlasting life." From that verse and many others in the Bible, we know that Jesus loves us and that He gave His life as a sacrifice on our behalf.

The scripture passage in John 3:16 immediately follows the report of Jesus' nighttime encounter with Nicodemus. In that meeting Jesus had explained that belief in Jesus would lead to spiritual rebirth, and that was essential for entrance into God's eternal kingdom. Understanding the events leading up to John 3:16 help us grasp the full measure of Jesus' message—a message of His extreme sacrificial love that leads to the indwelling of the Holy Spirit, which in turn leads to our living with God forever. So let's walk through the verses leading up to John 3:16.

At the outset of chapter 3, we learn that Nicodemus was a Pharisee and a member of the Sanhedrin, the Jewish governing body (John 3:1). He'd been impressed by the miracles performed by Jesus during the Passover Festival, and Nicodemus understood those to be signs from God (John 2:23; 3:2). But he did not understand the message of Jesus, so he came for a one-on-one meeting. He came secretly, under cover of darkness, so that his reputation for having all the answers would not be undercut and so that he would not be disparaged for associating with Jesus.

That was when Jesus said that one must be born again—born of the Spirit—in order to enter eternal life in God's Kingdom (John 3:3–8). Being born of the Spirit is a reference to receiving the powerful influence of the Holy Spirit that was sent as our counselor after Jesus' death, resurrection, and ascension. (See John 14:16–20 for Jesus' description of the Spirit, and see Titus 3:5–7 and 1 Peter 1:3–4 for an overview of our being reborn in the Spirit which leads to eternal life). When we look to Jesus as our savior and make Him Lord over our life by following the Holy Spirit's direction, we are reborn, i.e., we become a new creation (2 Corinthians 5:17).

Understandably, Nicodemus was confused. So Jesus explained in Old Testament terms that would be familiar to Nicodemus. The Old Testament, after all, was a foreshadowing of things to come. Jesus used the scripture from Numbers 21:4–9 to explain the concept of being saved by looking in faith to the Messiah for life.

In the passage from Numbers, the chosen people had turned against God; they were cursing their exodus from Egypt. They'd become "snake-bitten" with sin and that manifested in the form of venomous snakes that bit and killed many of the people in the group. In response to Moses's prayer, God instructed Moses to fashion a bronze snake wrapped around a pole so that anyone who "beheld" the figure on the pole would live (Numbers 21:8–9).

While the snake had represented sin since the time of Adam and Eve, bronze had represented judgment and sacrifice, as evidence by the bronze altar and bronze implements for sin offerings prescribed in Exodus 27:1-5 and 35:16. Jesus explained to Nicodemus that judgment and punishment for the guilt of mankind would take place on a pole—the cross—and all who looked to Jesus for their redemption would be saved. Jesus put it this way, "Just as Moses lifted up the snake in the wilderness, so the Son of Man must be lifted up, [so] that everyone who believes may have eternal life" (John 3:14–15).

We know from history that Jesus in fact was lifted up on the cross (John 12:32). And scripture tells us, "If we declare with our mouth that Jesus is Lord and believe in our heart that God raised Him from the dead then we will be saved" (Romans 10:9). The nighttime meeting between Jesus and Nicodemus provided instruction about Jesus' great love for us that would cause Him to be lifted on the cross to suffer judgment on our behalf. All who would look to Him would receive new life brought on by the Holy Spirit.

By looking to Jesus, we receive the Holy Spirit, and our life is forever changed (1 Corinthians 3:16). By looking to Jesus, we are reborn spiritually; the Holy Spirit takes up residence within us and seals us for eternal life. And John 3:16 is a succinct statement encapsulating the complex concept that we are loved so much that Jesus served our death sentence and gave us new and lasting life by implanting God's Holy Spirit in the souls of believers.

The sacrifice that Jesus bore on our behalf is proof of His extraordinary love for us. Jesus instructed, "Greater love has no man than this: that he would lay down his life for his friends" (John 15:13). And once God's plan for salvation had been revealed, Jesus regarded all who accepted His sacrificial gift to be His friends (John 15:14).

Christ's extreme love for us is unmistakably shown by His suffering on our behalf. So consider if you will these questions for introspection:

1. Because Jesus loves us, He went to the cross on our behalf. How are you expressing gratitude for His loving sacrifice?
2. Because Jesus loves us, He arranged for God's Holy Spirit to take up residence within the hearts of believers. What steps are you taking to listen for the Spirit's direction in your life?
3. Because Jesus loves us, we can look to Jesus as our savior. How are you acknowledging Jesus as your Lord and Savior?

Jesus loved us so much that He bled, suffered, and died on the cross so that we could look to Him as atonement for our sins and as the agent for ushering God's Holy Spirit into our life. Receiving His Spirit changes us. We are reborn, and we become a changed person because of Jesus' love for us.

Jesus' love for us is a precious gift. Each of us is free to accept that gift, or we can reject it. Know that Jesus loves you, and He went to extreme measures to bring you the benefits of that precious love.

JESUS INSTRUCTS US TO LOVE OTHERS

John 13:34–35

A house is no stronger than its foundation. Jesus concluded His Sermon on the Mount with that very point. A house built upon a solid foundation will withstand the storms of this world. But a house built on the shifting sands of current culture will collapse as soon as the whims of society change (see Matthew 7:24–27).

Jesus built His ministry upon an unchanging principle: "A new command I give you: love one another. As I have loved you, so you must love one another. By this everyone will know that you are my disciples, if you love one another" (John 13:34–35). Loving others is an unchanging foundation of Christianity.

The Gospel writer John never lost sight of the fact that love was at the core of Jesus' ministry. In 1 John chapter 4, John laid out a syllogism explaining the command to love one another. He started with the proposition that love comes from God (1 John 4:7). In fact, he defined God as love (1 John 4:8, 16). He next postulated that everyone who loves has come from God—love is a characteristic that has been passed down to us from God. And God demonstrated His love for us by sending His Son, Jesus, to bring lasting life to God's creations (1 John 4:7–9). To that he added God loved us by sending His Son as the atoning sacrifice for our sin before we loved Him (1 John 4:10). John concluded, therefore, "since God so loved us, we also ought to love one another" (1 John 4:11).

John's logic is easy to hear but difficult to follow. Of course, Jesus loved us. Look at what He did. He laid down His life so that you and I could live eternally in Heaven. But He died for sinners, i.e., for those who were opposing God! "Forgive them," he gasped, using His fleeting human strength to pray for those who nailed Him to the cross (Luke 23:34).

The love that Jesus demonstrated was difficult. Jesus' death on our behalf was not "easy love." At the time of Moses, God began with easy love: "Love your neighbor as yourself" was God's direction (Leviticus 19:18). But Jesus introduced the next level of love. "You've heard it said, 'love your neighbor'…but I tell you love your enemies" (Matthew 5:43–44).

The firm foundation of our spiritual house is built on love—love that extends to those who oppose us and to those who seek to destroy things that we hold dear. Jesus died for sinners—for those who opposed God. That kind of love is greater than feelings of affection for those who think the same as we do or who live next door. Christ's love is lasting because it is not dependent on the whims of other people.

Jesus came to teach us that next level of love. He explained, "greater love has no one than this: to lay down His life for his friends" (John 15:13). Jesus considered His friends to be all who would accept His death as cover for their sins and follow Christ's plan for salvation. Jesus lived out His teaching by dying on the cross for sinners. His love extended to those who had defied godly principles by living contrary to God's inspired teachings in scripture. Love at Jesus' level was love that extended to all.

You and I are called to love like Jesus loved. Easy love is a starting place—easy love includes the feelings we have for those who are within the scope of our natural affection. But when Jesus said that Christians would be known by their love, He was talking about the kind of love that He demonstrated. He was talking about loving our enemies. He was talking about Republicans loving Democrats and vice versa. He was talking about liberals and conservatives finding common ground by honestly listening to the perspective of others. He was talking about nonjudgmental dialogue about godly living.

Jesus saw hope for repentance and changed lives for those who previously had been drawn into Satan's worldly traps. But loving our enemies is no easy task because love sometimes means sharing hard truths. Lovingly sharing scripture means speaking the truth but without judgment (Ephesians 4:15). Jesus died for us while we were still sinners, before we repented (Romans 5:8).

So is your spiritual house built on the decision to love others—to love even those who seem unlovable to our worldly thinking? Consider these questions for introspection if you will:

1. Loving as Jesus loved means loving even the unlovable. Who would that be for you?
2. How can you demonstrate God's love for those who defy the moral standards of scripture?
3. Love as Jesus taught is a decision, not a human emotion. What are you doing to strengthen your commitment to the kind of love that Jesus promoted?

God is love. The essence of loving God is to live with love for all His creation—even the unlovable. While love does not mean affirming the actions of those who defy God, neither does it mean standing in judgment. We need to discern the difference between godly living and the shifting sands of worldly culture, yet judgment is reserved for God.

Jesus set the example of taking love to the next level. Christians are known for their Christlike love. May we grow every day in Christian love.

JESUS FASTED THROUGH TEMPTATION

Matthew 4:1–4

During the Great Exodus, the Hebrew nation passed through the waters of the Red Sea and then entered a time of testing to see whether they would keep God's commands and heed His promises (Deuteronomy 8:2). They stumbled because they focused on the things of this world rather than keeping their eyes fixed on God's Word. And as a result, their learning time in the wilderness grew to forty years; one year for each of the forty days spent by the faithless scouting party that feared entering the territory of God's Promise (Numbers 14:34).

Once Jesus passed through the waters of His baptism, scripture says the Spirit immediately led Him into the wilderness where He was subjected to testing and temptations for forty days (Matthew 4:1–4). Jesus fasted, focusing intently on God's instructions and repressing the instinct to satisfy temporal hungers of this world. He succeeded in resisting Satan's temptations.

Today we consider the topic "fasting." How does this practice help us? Does fasting have a role in resisting temptation? Patterns in the Old Testament scriptures may offer clues. When Moses ascended Mount Horeb to receive God's law, Moses spent forty days and forty nights without eating any food or drinking any water (Exodus 34:28). He was intent on communing with God to learn spiritual insights for living. Similarly, when the prophet Elijah fled into the wilderness of Mount Horeb, he traveled forty days and forty nights without food and water, focusing solely on God's directions (1 Kings 19:8).

Moses and Elijah were tempted by earthly hungers and circumstances but practiced fasting—concentrating on the eternal to the exclusion of the things of this world. Satan worked through the Hebrew people to tempt Moses by rebelling and murmuring against him. Satan worked through the pagan prophets of Baal and Queen Jezebel to test Elijah. And when it came to Jesus, Satan cut out the middlemen and directly tempted Jesus himself. But have you noticed that each time that Satan's temptations were overcome, fasting was part of the solution?

As we enter the forty days of Lent, we are reminded of Jesus' fasting and the examples of Moses and Elijah, who did likewise. Jesus taught, "Blessed are those who hunger and thirst for righteousness, for they will be filled" (Matthew 5:6). Our human instinct is to satisfy our temporary body with worldly food and drink—sustenance from this realm. The examples of fasting, however, remind us, "We do not live by bread alone but by every word that comes from the mouth of God" (Matthew 4:4 where Jesus was quoting Deuteronomy 8:3).

Fasting, as demonstrated by Jesus and recorded in the book of Matthew, was not limited to abstaining from food and drink, but fasting included rejecting the things of this world that tend to puff us up like power or prestige. Jesus shunned Satan's promise of power, repelled the notion of testing God's love for Him and refused promises of material wealth (Matthew 4:4–9). Fasting can take various forms, but it involves giving up the satisfaction that comes from this world, so that we are nourished exclusively by the eternal things that feed our soul.

Our soul is fed when we meditate on God's Word, reading a line or two of scripture and then praying for God, through His Holy Spirit, to reveal its meaning to us. Our soul is fed when we pray by simply being silent, waiting on God to speak to us. Our spirit soars when we focus on things that are right, pure, holy, and true (see Philippians 4:8).

God is Spirit (John 4:24), and we are made in His image (Genesis 1:27). You and I are spiritual beings, temporarily housed in earthly bodies (2 Corinthians 5:1). We need to feed our spirit, and that is enhanced when we practice fasting—a practice that draws our attention away from this world's provisions and helps us focus on God's spiritual sustenance.

So consider these questions for introspection:

1. Testing and temptation are part of the learning process. When have you encoun-

tered a moral challenge or a temptation that required drawing on spiritual answers? What spiritual growth opportunity was being presented by this challenge?

2. Fasting not only requires depriving ourselves of earthly sustenance, it also necessitates shifting our focus to the spiritual realm. What steps can you take to concentrate your focus more intently on spiritual matters?

3. If we "do not live by bread alone, but on every word that comes from the mouth of God" then how are you serving up God's Word for yourself and your family?

By feeding our spiritual self, we are better poised to resist the temptations brought on by Satan. You and I are called to live in the spirit (Galatians 5:25). Our spiritual nature needs building up because our battles are with the spiritual forces of evil (Ephesians 6:12).

During this season of lent, consider the role of fasting. Facing temptations requires application of spiritual principles. When we feed on God's Word, and nothing else, spiritual principles guide our response to the temptations of this world.

RELATIONSHIP
WITH JESUS
John 15:1–8

One of the classic old-time hymns is "What a Friend We Have in Jesus."

> What a friend we have in Jesus
> All our sins and griefs to bear
> What a privilege to carry
> Everything to God in prayer

The hymn goes on to list various aspects of what it means to have a relationship with Jesus.

For the past couple of weeks, we've talked about basic building blocks of Christianity: prayer, scripture, and devotion time. Now we bring those building blocks together to talk about developing a meaningful relationship with Jesus.

Reading scripture is important. But reading and understanding scripture, without more, does not bring us into relationship with Jesus. After all, even the demons know scripture (see James 2:19). And prayers—those are two-way conversations involving sharing our heart with God and listening for a response—are essential to beginning to develop a relationship. But still more is required.

As mere mortals, we are incapable of leading lives perfect in every thought, word, and deed. For the sake of our eternal soul, we need not only accept Jesus as our savior, but also to develop a meaningful relationship with Jesus. So this week's topic is about developing a friendship and lasting relationship with our savior, Jesus. The assigned scripture is John 15:1–8.

James, the brother of Jesus, instructed that we are to be "doers of the Word" (James 1:22). The Gospel writer, John, explained that the Word was "in the beginning…the Word was with God…and the Word was God," and later "the Word became flesh and dwelt among us" (John 1:1–14). From that, we know that Jesus was and is the Word of God. If we are to be "doers of the Word," then how do we "do Jesus"?

Jesus, himself, provided the instructions for developing and maintaining a meaningful relationship with him. In John 15, Jesus uses the analogy that he is the vine and God is the gardener. As Christians, we are branches attached to the vine. We receive our nourishment and direction from the vine—from Jesus. When we accept Jesus as our savior, we receive the Holy Spirit. The Spirit lives within us and counsels us as we grow in love of Jesus and obedience to His teachings (John 14:15–17). By being attuned to the Holy Spirit flowing through us, we become more Christlike, allowing development of the fruit of the Spirit. The fruit of the Spirit is "love, joy, peace, forbearance, kindness, goodness, faithfulness, gentleness, and self-control" (Galatians 5:22).

Jesus explained that any branch (any person who claims to be a Christian) that bears no fruit is cut off and thrown into the fire (John 15:2, 6–7). People who claim to be Christians, but do not develop a relationship with Jesus, tend not to bear fruit. Today, many profess to be Christians but view Jesus' teachings as optional or unimportant. Some have "higher priorities" that prevent them from regularly reading their Bible or conversing with God through prayer. Some view their own reasoning as superior to the outdated standards specified by God in scripture.

Those who profess to be Christians but block any meaningful relationship with Jesus can distort the church and drag it off course. The gardener—God—cuts those branches off and tosses them into the fire.

But Jesus further explained that the branches bearing fruit are also pruned in order to improve the production of fruit (John 15:2). Christians who are striving to be ever closer in their walk with Jesus are subject to life's challenges and trials. Life circumstances can force us to adjust our attitude and increase our reliance on Jesus. Sometimes a calamity in finances or relationships will prompt us to rein-ventory our outlook, changing our priorities and improving our production of fruit of the spirit.

So how do we make and keep that connection to Jesus that generates Christian characteristics (fruit of the Spirit)? Let me suggest four steps:

(1) First, we need to acknowledge that we need a savior; we need Jesus. "All have sinned and fall short of the glory of God"

(Romans 3:23). We need Jesus in order to reach Heaven and to be in union with God. (John 14:6, "I am the way and the truth and the life. No one comes to the Father except through me.") In our prayer time we can declare Jesus as Lord over our life and savior of our soul. That brings His saving grace and allows His Holy Spirit to enter within us.

(2) The second step is for us to study scripture so that we understand that Jesus is who He said He is, i.e., the Son of God. When we study Jesus, we recognize Him as all-powerful, all Holy, the source and creator of everything.

(3) Third, we need to incorporate Jesus' teachings and example into our daily living. That is to say that we need to "do" the will of God as explained by Jesus. In Matthew 7:21, Jesus advised, "not everyone who says to me, 'Lord, Lord,' will enter the kingdom of heaven, but only the one who does the will of my Father." Similarly, when Jesus described the process of judgment, he stated that we would be judged on the basis of our actions in Christlike behavior (Matthew 25:40). A relationship with Jesus involves action, following the course that Jesus laid out for us.

(4) And fourth, we need to yield to Jesus in our every waking moment. Several years ago, a popular movement swept the country, causing many to wear WWJD wristbands—reminding them to ask throughout the day, "What would Jesus do" in this circumstance or in this conversation? We need to consider Jesus' direction in every thought, word, and deed throughout every day. That is to say, we need Jesus to be our first priority in every aspect of our life—Lord of our life.

So reflect with me for a moment, if you will. How is your relationship with Jesus?

1. Do you truly believe that you need a savior? Our human tendency is to believe that "I'm OK." I'm not robbing banks or cheating on my wife. Recognizing the need for a savior involves deep introspection, reflecting on the language we use, the thoughts that we harbor, the Christian actions that we avoid. If you were called to account for your life right now, where would you be vulnerable?

2. Have you declared Jesus to be Lord over all aspects of your life? What does that mean for you? Are there some parts of your life that you try to keep secret from

Jesus, not letting His instruction influence your actions?

3. And how are you yielding your everyday life to Jesus? What steps are you taking to build a meaningful relationship with Him? Quality relationships grow out of commitments of quantity time. How are you spending time with Jesus each day?

Developing a friendship with Jesus is essential. Each of us needs a savior because left to our own devises we fall short of God's standards for holiness. A meaningful relationship with Jesus requires a commitment of time and effort for prayer, scripture and actions. He promises that as we remain connected to Him, He remains in us and empowers us to accomplish His will (John 15:7). What a friend we have in Jesus!

JESUS IS MY SHEPHERD
John 10:1–10; Psalm 23

In the Gospel of John, Jesus analogized Himself to a shepherd, leading His flock—He was speaking of leading Christians, including you and me in everyday living. He explained that the only way to be part of His flock was by listening for His word and heeding His instructions. His followers recognize the voice of Jesus; they are attuned to His directions, and they follow only Him (John 10:1–5).

In today's world our attention is often diverted away from Jesus; we are led by other forces. Things of this world easily distract us and direct our course. We follow the stock market, we enthusiastically support our favorite sports teams, or we look to a political party or politician for answers rather than listen for Jesus' directions.

Then came the coronavirus pandemic. Faith in the stock market came crashing down. Sports—all sports—were cancelled. Political rallies were banned and even elections were jeopardized and delayed. So now who will we follow? Are the distractions taken away yet? Can we now focus our attention on Jesus and only Him?

The words of the venerable 23rd Psalm come to mind. "He leads me to green pastures beside still waters." And He leads me in paths of righteousness, for His name's sake. Even though I'm walking in the shadow of death, I'm at peace when I realize that He is walking with me. When I become still, listening for His leadership in my life, I return to the flock and His peace overcomes me (see, e.g., Philippians 4:7).

Now many of the false gods of this world have been shut down, and there is greater opportunity to rest in quiet spaces where we can hear Jesus—if we are seeking Him. This feels strange. We've grown accustomed to a world that is teaming with activity. But now streets are barren, rush hours are quiet, and social activities are closed.

Strange though it may feel, this is not a new circumstance. In 2 Chronicles, chapter 15, we read of a time when Israel strayed from God. Their attention had been diverted by the false gods of their time. Scripture says that in those days people could not even travel safely—sound familiar? The Bible records what happened, "But in their distress they turned to the Lord, the God of Israel, and sought Him, and He was found by them" (2 Chronicles 15:4–5).

There is a recurrent theme in Scripture: in times of distress—distress often brought on by our own waywardness—we can call on the Lord and He answers, making His presence known. He guides us on a path that brings us back to Him. Take a look, for example, at Psalm 120. It begins this way: "I call on the Lord in my distress, and He answers me" (Psalm 120:1). Psalm 121 continues the message: "Where does my help come from? My help comes from the Lord" (Psalm 121:2). That passage explains that our help comes from our Lord—Jesus—who is with us constantly, watching over us, never sleeping.

The reality is that throughout the contemporary world many have rejected Jesus. They've let sports displace time of worship. They've suggested that moral standards are better set by politicians than by God. They've repressed public mention of the name of Jesus, rationalizing that religion is a private matter that should be hidden under a basket. (To the contrary, see Matthew 5:14–15.)

The coronavirus pandemic has not taken God by surprise. Rather, this appears to be yet another instance of mankind having drifted away from God, following the voice of earthly false shepherds. Suddenly we realize that we've left His flock and have strayed into a domain that brings pain, suffering, and death. In our distress, we need to seek our true shepherd, Jesus. Returning our focus to Him brings us to calm spots—green pastures and still waters. He is always there for us. He will never leave us (Deuteronomy 31:6, Matthew 28:20, Hebrews 13:5).

So reflect with me, if you will, on these questions for introspection:

1. In recent times (before the coronavirus pandemic), what forces have been leading your life?
2. How has your response to the coronavirus pandemic forced you into a quiet place?

3. What adjustments are you making in your life in order to be better able to hear Jesus' message for His leadership in your life?

Once again, the world has been drawn into a season of distress. Perhaps it's no coincidence that this period of distress coincides with a time when earthly forces have been drawing us away from God. In times of turmoil, Jesus is present, leading us to quiet places, drawing us to opportunities for reflection. This is when we need to pay particular attention to the one true shepherd who leads us on the path of godly living.

During His ministry, Jesus admonished us not to worry about worldly circumstances—concerns like the stock market, the March Madness basketball tournaments, and the deadlock of Washington, DC. We are to vigilantly resist following the false shepherds of this world that are constantly tugging on our lives. We are to seek first God's Kingdom—His plans and priorities—then all our needs and concerns will be met (Matthew 6:33).

Jesus is the Good Shepherd. May we slow down and allow Him to lead us to quiet places where we are more apt to hear His call and heed His direction. Jesus is the only true shepherd.

JESUS INSTRUCTS US TO MENTOR

John 14:1–14

66 "In my Father's house there are many rooms. If it were not so, I would have told you. And I'm going there to prepare a place for you." Those words of comfort from the Gospel of John, 14:1–3, are spoken at many funeral services. They are a reminder that Jesus has arranged a place in Heaven for each of us. Home is ready and waiting for those who put their faith in Jesus (Romans 10:9).

Jesus instructed that whoever believes in Him will continue the works that Jesus did during His ministry on earth. Those works include teaching God's principles for daily living. Works done in the name of Jesus, i.e., works that are in keeping with Jesus' nature and character will be blessed (John 14:12–14).

Believing in Jesus and working like He did does not come spontaneously. These are learned behaviors. Ideally, believing in Jesus and continuing His works begin at the earliest stages of childhood. The wisdom of King Solomon includes the familiar admonition, "Train up a child in the ways he should go and when he is old he will not depart from it" (Proverbs 22:6).

Mothers not only give birth to their children; they nurture and teach them so that one day their child is independent and able to continue the cycle of life by nurturing his or her own children.

The parenting role we recognize today often rests on the shoulders of mothers, but frankly, it's a role that each of us is called to fulfill. As Christians, you and I are in a position to provide the tools and role modeling that enable the next generation to believe in Jesus and to continue His ministry.

Jesus explained to Nicodemus that believing in Jesus and His ministry is a matter of being "born again" (John 3:3). New Christians are like newborn babies; they need mothering. They need bonding and fellowship like that given by a mother to her newborn child. New Christians require role models and teachers so that they can follow the teachings of Jesus, understand His ways, and form a deeper relationship with Him. New Christians, in the usual cycle of life, mature so that they become independent of their early mentors and become mentors for other new Christians.

The Great Commission calls on Christians to make disciples of all nations (Matthew 28:19). That means that each of us has a mentoring role, a responsibility to nurture the next generations of believers. In Old Testament times, parents were instructed to "impress [God's commandments] on your children. Talk about [the commandments continuously]" (Deuteronomy 6:7). Similarly, the

New Testament instructs us to teach and model the ways of Christ for the next generation of believers (Titus 2:1–8).

Making disciples involves mentoring others. So consider these questions for introspection:

1. All of us are called to teach and model God's ways for the next generation of believers. What steps are you taking to influence and teach new believers?

2. Part of the teaching process outlined in Deuteronomy 6:8–9 is to demonstrate our beliefs in God by displaying them on our doorframes, gateposts, and even on ourselves. What outward demonstrations are you making to model Christian beliefs to the world?

3. A mentor's role includes a time of "letting go" so that the next generation can stand on the Christian principles they've learned and live out their responsibilities for building the Kingdom of Christ. How are you turning over the reins for Christian leadership to the next generation?

Mentoring the next generation is not an easy role. Children sometimes rebel and reject instruction. Nevertheless, laying a firm foundation for Christian newborns is part of the life cycle. And teaching principles for Christian living is necessary to achieve the homecoming that Jesus introduced in John's Gospel.

So let's all shoulder the responsibility to teach and
model Christian principles for the next generation of
believers.

ALIVE WITH CHRIST

Ephesians 2:1–10

Today we consider what it means to be "alive with Christ" and we'll talk about how that condition occurs. The apostle Paul explained to the new believers in Ephesus, "You were [once] dead in your transgressions and sin… when you followed the ways of this world" but "by grace you have been saved," "made alive with Christ" (Ephesians 2:1–5).

Our perspective on life depends on the source to which we look for meaning in our life. If we define ourselves by temporal characteristics of wealth, power, and prestige, then we are never satisfied because these conditions are fleeting and unreliable. By seeking value from earthly sources, we are doomed to suffer under the curse of limited resources and hard times that are a by-product of our sinful and self-centered nature (Genesis 3:17–23). Moreover, by looking to this world for meaning, we are locked into the endless struggle of wrestling with the law that separates good and evil and ultimately leads to death (Romans 6:23).

But if we look to Jesus as the source of meaning for our lives, we can rise above earthly limitations. When Jesus is our Lord, we see His creation around every corner and in every person we meet. We see potential for good and we have hope in things yet unseen (Hebrews 11:1). The Holy Spirit takes up residence within us and calls us into God's intended plan (1 Corinthians 3:16; 2 Corinthians 5:16–17). This condition is what the apostle Paul referred to as being "alive with Christ" (Ephesians 2:5).

We live in a world that teaches, "There is no free lunch." Our mindset is "if we want to receive something of value, we must work for it." While this work ethic has general application to life experiences of this world, it does not fit the spiritual gift of being made alive with Christ.

Yet many Christians try to earn the gift of being alive with Christ. They toil in mission activities or they volunteer for every church-related work in hopes of earning Christ's gift. But being made alive with Christ is not something that we earn. It is a gift that is freely given by Jesus. Once we've accepted the gift of Jesus' righteousness as our own, then we become a changed person (2 Corinthians 5:17). Then we are employed in performing the good works that God has planned for us (Ephesians 2:10).

Paul wrote that all believers are "alive with Christ" (Ephesians 2:5). He explained, "God, who has great love for us and who is rich in mercy, made us alive with Christ even when we were dead in transgressions. It is by grace that we have been saved" (Ephesians 2:4–5). He employed similar language when he wrote to the church in Colossae (Colossians 2:13). Being alive with Christ is the product of Jesus' sacrifice on the cross—a gift of God. It is not something that we can earn by our worldly efforts.

Years ago I was meeting with the renowned evangelist, Harald Bredesen, trying to prepare him for a deposition that was planned in a pending lawsuit. Bredesen had a different objective for our meeting. He interrupted my explanation of the legal process with what to him was a more pressing issue. "If you died at this very moment and were met by Saint Peter at the pearly gates of Heaven, what would you tell him that would cause him to open the gate for your admission into Heaven?"

I fumbled for an answer to his question. "I would tell him that I've taught Sunday school for many years and that I've held various posts in the church."

He nodded and I continued with my explanation of the legal issues. After a moment, however, it occurred to me how badly I had answered his question. "Wait a minute," I said, "there is nothing I can do to earn my admission into Heaven. That was done by Jesus' death on the cross to cover my sins."

At that, Bredesen let out a whoop. "Praise Jesus!" Then he was able to focus on the issues presented in the pending lawsuit.

Salvation is a gift. While we were still sinners, Christ died for us so that His righteousness became ours (Romans 5:8, 2 Corinthians 5:21). But being alive with Christ is not limited to our afterlife. Jesus came to give life in abundance even during our time on earth (John 10:10). Before we accept the gift of forgiveness of our sin debt, we are "dead men walking." We are on our own, doing the best we can in Satan's minefields of deception and danger.

But once we accept Jesus' kingship over our soul, the Holy Spirit takes up residence and counsels us in Christlike actions (John 14:15–18). Holy Spirit guides us on the course of life that God planned for us from before the time we were knit together in our mother's womb (Jeremiah 1:5). The strength of the Holy Spirit within us "is greater than he who is in the world" (1 John 4:4). Therefore, as recipients of the Holy Spirit, we have the power to overcome the challenges we face in this world.

Accordingly, we see that being alive with Christ cannot be earned. It is an undeserved blessing—an act of grace—freely given through Jesus' death on the cross to cover us with His righteousness. Paul expressed it this way: "God made Him who had no sin to be sin for us, so that in Him we might become the righteousness of God" (2 Corinthians 5:21). Being alive with Christ begins right here on earth when we give Jesus the reigns to our life. That's when our perspective changes; that's when we derive meaning for our life by realizing that we are citizens of God's kingdom.

So reflect with me if you will on the following questions for introspection:

1. Being "alive with Christ" occurs when the Holy Spirit takes up residence within us to lead and guide us in our everyday living. How are you listening for Holy Spirit's direction in your life?

2. Jesus died to cover our sins and to make way for Holy Spirit to enter each of us. Are you trying to earn your relationship

with Jesus, or have you accepted His free gift? How can you tell the difference?

3. If governing our life by the dictates of law is deadly, then what should be our standard for living? Does that mean that we disregard the standards God imposed in the law?

God, in His mercy, has made believers "alive with Christ" (Ephesians 2:5). All of us have sinned in thought, word, or deed, and therefore our just recompense is death according to Romans 6:23. But while we were still sinners, Jesus died on our behalf, paying the penalty for our sin (Romans 5:8). When we accept His free gift, we experience life in a new way. We recognize His creation and direction in each of the scenarios that play out in our life. We yearn to live like Jesus and therefore listen for the Spirit's leading that takes us away from sin and deception. Service becomes a fruit rather than a work. As new creations in Christ, we view the world from the perspective of citizens of Heaven. Welcome the Spirit's leading and experience being alive with Christ!

ABOUT THE AUTHOR

Although he claims no credentials as a theologian, Glen Huff has long studied scripture and sought to understand its application to everyday life. A decade ago, he published *Daily Devotional*. He practiced law for nearly thirty-five years before becoming a judge on the Court of Appeals of Virginia where he continues to sit.

Growing up in a family of modest means in rural Maine, Huff experienced a gnawing curiosity about many things that once seemed out of reach. As a university student he learned to fly, interned for a US senator who was running for president, and played violin in the orchestra. But nothing taught him more about scripture's application to everyday life than the abrupt closing of the law firm in which he was first employed.

He and his wife, Linda, have been married nearly fifty years and are blessed with two children, Jeremy Huff (married to Janice) and Laura Mack (married to Ryan), and two wonderful grandchildren with more on the way.

CPSIA information can be obtained
at www.ICGtesting.com
Printed in the USA
BVHW032209190222
629584BV00005B/194